YOUR

CANCER

JOURNAL

TRACK SYMPTOMS & SIDE EFFECTS

PAIN AND ENERGY TRACKER

MEDICATION AND SUPPLEMENT TRACKER

TIME OF DAY PAIN SCALES

GRATITUDE PROMPTS & BEAUTIFUL QUOTES

MOOD TRACKING FOR MENTAL HEALTH & MINDFULNESS PROMPTS

KEEP MEDICAL NOTES AND SHOW YOUR DOCTOR

JOURNAL

...and much more!

This journal is thoughtfully made to help track your treatment, illness, mental health, symptoms, keep track of pain and energy levels.

There are also **food logs and food trigger tracking.** Use to take to doctors appointments. write down your thoughts and feelings with regards to your pain,treatment and more. With gratitude prompts to refocus you on bad days to why life is great! As well as self esteem exercises, mindfulness prompts, beautiful illustrations and quotes!

This book is also a journal with many lined pages.

Wishing you luck and love on your journey.

DAILY ENERGY vs MOOD TRACKER

TRACK YOUR DAILY ENERGY, MOOD AND ALSO PAIN USING DIFFERENT COLOURS ON THIS LINE CHART

100

75

50

25

0   MONDAY   TUESDAY   WEDNESDAY   THURSDAY   FRIDAY   SATURDAY   SUNDAY

ENERGY

PAIN

TIME OF DAY PAIN TRACKER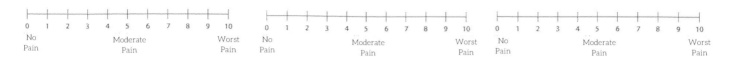

MORNING

| 0 | 1 | 2 | 3 | 4 | 5 | 6 | 7 | 8 | 9 | 10 |

No Pain   Moderate Pain   Worst Pain

AFTERNOON

| 0 | 1 | 2 | 3 | 4 | 5 | 6 | 7 | 8 | 9 | 10 |

No Pain   Moderate Pain   Worst Pain

EVENING

| 0 | 1 | 2 | 3 | 4 | 5 | 6 | 7 | 8 | 9 | 10 |

No Pain   Moderate Pain   Worst Pain

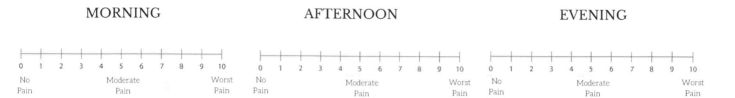

MORNING

AFTERNOON

EVENING

No Pain   Moderate Pain   Worst Pain

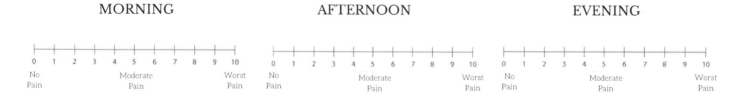

MORNING

AFTERNOON

EVENING

No Pain   Moderate Pain   Worst Pain

MORNING

AFTERNOON

EVENING

No Pain   Moderate Pain   Worst Pain

MORNING

AFTERNOON

EVENING

No Pain   Moderate Pain   Worst Pain

SYMPTOM & TRIGGER TRACKER

	FREQ. / SEVERITY Y/N	MON	TUES	WED	THURS	FRI	SAT	SUN
DID YOU HAVE A GOOD DAY? (YES NO, 0-5 BAD TO GOOD)	Y/N 0-5	☐	☐	☐	☐	☐	☐	☐
MUSCLE PAIN OR WEAKNESS	0-5							
JOINT PAIN	0-5							
ENERGY LEVELS	0-5							
ANXIETY	0-5							
DIFFICULTY SLEEPING	0-5							
FEELING DEPRESSED / LOW MOOD	0-5							
OVER SLEEPING	Y/N							
DROWSIENESS	0-5							
HEADACHE / MIGRAINE	Y/N							
NAUSEA	0-5							
DIARRHOEA	0-5							
CONSTIPATION	Y-N							
BLOATING	0-5							
ACID REFLUX	Y/N							
NUMBNESS OR TINGLING	0-5							
HAIR LOSS	0-5							
SWOLLEN LYMPH NODES	0-5							
HEART PALPITATIONS	Y/N							
DRY EYES OR VISION PROBLEMS	0-5							
RINGING IN EARS	Y/N							
SENSITIVITY TO LIGHT	0-5							
SENSITIVITY TO SOUND	Y/N							
FACIAL NUMBNESS	Y/N							
BRAIN FOG / DIFFICULTY CONCENTRATING	Y/N							
HEADACHE OR MIGRAINE	Y/N							

CONTINUE TO THE NEXT PAGE

SYMPTOM & TRIGGER TRACKER

	FREQ. / SEVERITY Y/N	MON	TUES	WED	THURS	FRI	SAT	SUN
EXERCISE	MINS							
RASH	0-5							
MOUTH SORES	Y/N							
SKIN RASH	0-5							
UTI, DARK URINE OR OTHER BLADDER ISSUES	0-5							
LOW GRADE FEVER	TEMP							
COLD OR INFECTION	Y/N							
SHORTNESS OF BREATH	Y/N							
MEDICATION:	DOSE	☐	☐	☐	☐	☐	☐	☐
MEDICATION:	DOSE							
MEDICATION:	DOSE							
MEDICATION:	DOSE							

FILL IN THE CHARTS TO TRACK SYMPTOMS AND THEN PUT DETAILS AND POST POSSIBLE TRIGGERS IN THE NOTES BELOW.

_____
_____
_____
_____
_____
_____
_____
_____
_____
_____
_____
_____

HOW OFTEN DID YOU FILL OUT THIS CHART

NOT AT ALL   [ ]   1-3X PER WEEK   [ ]   ALMOST EVERY DAY   [ ]   EVERYDAY   [ ]

SYMPTOM TRACKER

DATE	TIME	DURATION	DESCRIPTION
8/30			Day of 1st Infusion - no symptoms but tired
9/1			mild Headache all day, by evening itchy skin + hot flashes, skin feeling hot bothering me a lot.
9/5 - 9/9			on + off itchy - one day head very itchy + hot skin - not constant
9-8			night time pain began in left leg + hip - very uncomfortable hard to sleep.
~~9~~			
9.9			Pain ok - walked then in early afternoon same leg pain again
9.20			Tired + went to bed @ 8:30 after the 2:30 infusion - no pain that day

TIME OF DAY SYMPTOM TRACKER

TRACK THE SEVERITY OF YOUR SYMPTOMS THROUGHOUT THE DAY USING THE SCALE, USE THE NOTE SECTION BELOW TO LIST THE SYMPTOMS YOU EXPERIENCED. USE THIS TO SEE IF CERTAIN TIMES OF DAY E.G. MEAL TIMES OR FIRST THING IN THE MORNING, ARE TRIGGERS FOR YOU.

iad. nfusion afternoon 9/20

9/21

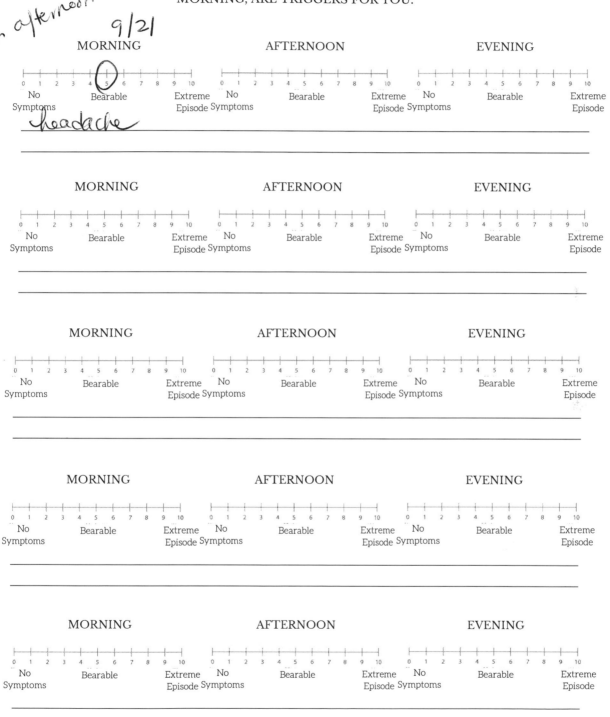

headache

MORNING	AFTERNOON	EVENING
0 1 2 3 4 5 6 7 8 9 10	0 1 2 3 4 5 6 7 8 9 10	0 1 2 3 4 5 6 7 8 9 10
No Symptoms — Bearable — Extreme Episode	No Symptoms — Bearable — Extreme Episode	No Symptoms — Bearable — Extreme Episode

PAIN TRACKER BAR CHART

1 ....

2

3 ....

4

5 ....

6

7

8 ....

9

10

MONDAY	TUESDAY	WEDNESDAY	THURSDAY	FRIDAY	SATURDAY	SUNDAY

FOOD LOG AND FOOD TRIGGER TRACKER

FOOD	AMOUNT	TIME	IMMEDIATELY AFTER	1 HOUR	3 HOURS

LOG HOW YOU FEEL AFTER FOOD IN THESE SECTIONS

FOOD TRACKER

MEAL	MONDAY	TUESDAY	WEDNESDAY	THURSDAY	FRIDAY	SATURDAY	SUNDAY
BREAKFAST							
LUNCH							
DINNER							
CALORIES (OPTIONAL)							
SUPPLEMENTS	MULTIVIT ☐ VITAMIN D ☐ CALCIUM ☐	MULTIVIT ☐ VITAMIN D ☐ CALCIUM ☐	MULTIVIT ☐ VITAMIN D ☐ CALCIUM ☐	MULTIVIT ☐ VITAMIN D ☐ CALCIUM ☐	MULTIVIT ☐ VITAMIN D ☐ CALCIUM ☐	MULTIVIT ☐ VITAMIN D ☐ CALCIUM ☐	MULTIVIT ☐ VITAMIN D ☐ CALCIUM ☐
WATER INTAKE	☐☐☐ ☐☐☐	☐☐☐ ☐☐☐	☐☐☐ ☐☐☐	☐☐☐ ☐☐☐	☐☐☐ ☐☐☐	☐☐☐ ☐☐☐	☐☐☐ ☐☐☐

EXERCISE	MONDAY	TUESDAY	WEDNESDAY	THURSDAY	FRIDAY	SATURDAY	SUNDAY

FILL IN THE NOTES BELOW ON AREAS FOR IMPROVEMENT, SHOPPING LISTS, HOW YOU FELT AFTER YOU ATE, CALORIES, SNACKS AND WHATEVER YOU THINK WOULD BE USEFUL TO ADD TO YOUR FOOD JOURNAL

_____
_____
_____
_____
_____
_____
_____
_____
_____

HOW OFTEN DID YOU FILL OUT THIS CHART
NOT AT ALL   [ ]   1-3X PER WEEK   [ ]   ALMOST EVERY DAY   [ ]   EVERYDAY   [ ]

MEDICATION & SUPPLEMENT TRACKER

MEDICATION NAME	DOSE.	MON	TUES	WED	THURS	FRI	SAT	SUN
EXAMPLE	5mg							

_____

_____

_____

_____

_____

_____

_____

One Minute Meditation

Breathe in through your nose.

Breathe out through your mouth.

Feel air in the depths of your lungs
as you breathe in again.

As you breathe out feel tension
release from your body.

Repeat 3x.

WHAT DOES GRATITUDE MEAN?

ANSWER THESE QUESTIONS TO BREAK OUT OF NEGATIVE THOUGHT PATTERNS AND REFOCUS ON THE THINGS THAT MAKE YOU HAPPY AND GRATEFUL.

_____

_____

_____

_____

_____

_____

_____

_____

_____

_____

_____

_____

_____

_____

_____

_____

_____

_____

_____

_____

DAILY ENERGY vs MOOD TRACKER

TRACK YOUR DAILY ENERGY, MOOD AND ALSO PAIN USING DIFFERENT COLOURS ON THIS LINE CHART

100

75

50

25

0

ENERGY

| MONDAY | TUESDAY | WEDNESDAY | THURSDAY | FRIDAY | SATURDAY | SUNDAY |

PAIN

TIME OF DAY PAIN TRACKER

MORNING

0 1 2 3 4 5 6 7 8 9 10

No   Moderate   Worst
Pain   Pain   Pain

AFTERNOON

0 1 2 3 4 5 6 7 8 9 10

No   Moderate   Worst
Pain   Pain   Pain

EVENING

0 1 2 3 4 5 6 7 8 9 10

No   Moderate   Worst
Pain   Pain   Pain

MORNING

0 1 2 3 4 5 6 7 8 9 10

No   Moderate   Worst
Pain   Pain   Pain

AFTERNOON

0 1 2 3 4 5 6 7 8 9 10

No   Moderate   Worst
Pain   Pain   Pain

EVENING

0 1 2 3 4 5 6 7 8 9 10

No   Moderate   Worst
Pain   Pain   Pain

MORNING

0 1 2 3 4 5 6 7 8 9 10

No   Moderate   Worst
Pain   Pain   Pain

AFTERNOON

0 1 2 3 4 5 6 7 8 9 10

No   Moderate   Worst
Pain   Pain   Pain

EVENING

0 1 2 3 4 5 6 7 8 9 10

No   Moderate   Worst
Pain   Pain   Pain

MORNING

0 1 2 3 4 5 6 7 8 9 10

No   Moderate   Worst
Pain   Pain   Pain

AFTERNOON

0 1 2 3 4 5 6 7 8 9 10

No   Moderate   Worst
Pain   Pain   Pain

EVENING

0 1 2 3 4 5 6 7 8 9 10

No   Moderate   Worst
Pain   Pain   Pain

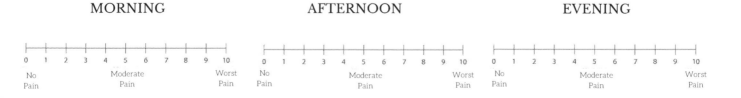

MORNING

0 1 2 3 4 5 6 7 8 9 10

No   Moderate   Worst
Pain   Pain   Pain

AFTERNOON

0 1 2 3 4 5 6 7 8 9 10

No   Moderate   Worst
Pain   Pain   Pain

EVENING

0 1 2 3 4 5 6 7 8 9 10

No   Moderate   Worst
Pain   Pain   Pain

SYMPTOM & TRIGGER TRACKER

	FREQ. / SEVERITY Y/N	MON	TUES	WED	THURS	FRI	SAT	SUN
DID YOU HAVE A GOOD DAY? (YES NO, 0-5 BAD TO GOOD)	Y/N 0-5	☐	☐	☐	☐	☐	☐	☐
MUSCLE PAIN OR WEAKNESS	0-5							
JOINT PAIN	0-5							
ENERGY LEVELS	0-5							
ANXIETY	0-5							
DIFFICULTY SLEEPING	0-5							
FEELING DEPRESSED / LOW MOOD	0-5							
OVER SLEEPING	Y/N							
DROWSIENESS	0-5							
HEADACHE / MIGRAINE	Y/N							
NAUSEA	0-5							
DIARRHOEA	0-5							
CONSTIPATION	Y-N							
BLOATING	0-5							
ACID REFLUX	Y/N							
NUMBNESS OR TINGLING	0-5							
HAIR LOSS	0-5							
SWOLLEN LYMPH NODES	0-5							
HEART PALPITATIONS	Y/N							
DRY EYES OR VISION PROBLEMS	0-5							
RINGING IN EARS	Y/N							
SENSITIVITY TO LIGHT	0-5							
SENSITIVITY TO SOUND	Y/N							
FACIAL NUMBNESS	Y/N							
BRAIN FOG / DIFFICULTY CONCENTRATING	Y/N							
HEADACHE OR MIGRAINE	Y/N							

CONTINUE TO THE NEXT PAGE

SYMPTOM & TRIGGER TRACKER

	FREQ. / SEVERITY Y/N	MON	TUES	WED	THURS	FRI	SAT	SUN
EXERCISE	MINS							
RASH	0-5							
MOUTH SORES	Y/N							
SKIN RASH	0-5							
UTI, DARK URINE OR OTHER BLADDER ISSUES	0-5							
LOW GRADE FEVER	TEMP							
COLD OR INFECTION	Y/N							
SHORTNESS OF BREATH	Y/N							
MEDICATION:	DOSE							
MEDICATION:	DOSE							
MEDICATION:	DOSE							
MEDICATION:	DOSE							

FILL IN THE CHARTS TO TRACK SYMPTOMS AND THEN PUT DETAILS AND POST POSSIBLE TRIGGERS IN THE NOTES BELOW.

_____

_____

_____

_____

_____

_____

_____

_____

_____

_____

_____

_____

_____

HOW OFTEN DID YOU FILL OUT THIS CHART

NOT AT ALL   [ ]   1-3X PER WEEK   [ ]   ALMOST EVERY DAY   [ ]   EVERYDAY   [ ]

SYMPTOM TRACKER

DATE	TIME	DURATION	DESCRIPTION
DATE	TIME	DURATION	DESCRIPTION

TIME OF DAY SYMPTOM TRACKER

TRACK THE SEVERITY OF YOUR SYMPTOMS THROUGHOUT THE DAY USING THE
SCALE, USE THE NOTE SECTION BELOW TO LIST THE SYMPTOMS YOU EXPERIENCED.
USE THIS TO SEE IF CERTAIN TIMES OF DAY E.G. MEAL TIMES OR FIRST THING IN THE
MORNING, ARE TRIGGERS FOR YOU.

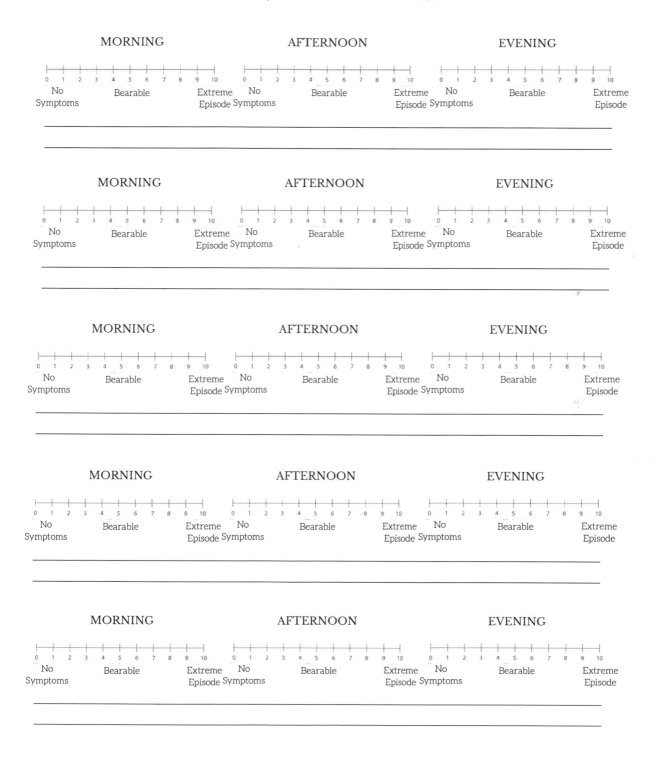

PAIN TRACKER BAR CHART

1
2
3
4
5
6
7
8
9
10

| MONDAY | TUESDAY | WEDNESDAY | THURSDAY | FRIDAY | SATURDAY | SUNDAY |

FOOD LOG AND FOOD TRIGGER TRACKER

FOOD	AMOUNT	TIME	IMMEDIATELY AFTER	1 HOUR	3 HOURS

LOG HOW YOU FEEL AFTER FOOD IN THESE SECTIONS

FOOD TRACKER

MEAL	MONDAY	TUESDAY	WEDNESDAY	THURSDAY	FRIDAY	SATURDAY	SUNDAY
BREAKFAST							
LUNCH							
DINNER							
CALORIES (OPTIONAL)							
SUPPLEMENTS	MULTIVIT ☐ VITAMIN D ☐ CALCIUM ☐	MULTIVIT ☐ VITAMIN D ☐ CALCIUM ☐	MULTIVIT ☐ VITAMIN D ☐ CALCIUM ☐	MULTIVIT ☐ VITAMIN D ☐ CALCIUM ☐	MULTIVIT ☐ VITAMIN D ☐ CALCIUM ☐	MULTIVIT ☐ VITAMIN D ☐ CALCIUM ☐	MULTIVIT ☐ VITAMIN D ☐ CALCIUM ☐
WATER INTAKE	☐☐☐ ☐☐☐	☐☐☐☐ ☐☐☐☐	☐☐☐☐ ☐☐☐☐	☐☐☐☐ ☐☐☐☐	☐☐☐☐ ☐☐☐☐	☐☐☐ ☐☐☐	☐☐☐ ☐☐☐

EXERCISE	MONDAY	TUESDAY	WEDNESDAY	THURSDAY	FRIDAY	SATURDAY	SUNDAY

FILL IN THE NOTES BELOW ON AREAS FOR IMPROVEMENT, SHOPPING LISTS, HOW YOU FELT AFTER YOU ATE, CALORIES, SNACKS AND WHATEVER YOU THINK WOULD BE USEFUL TO ADD TO YOUR FOOD JOURNAL

_____
_____
_____
_____
_____
_____
_____
_____
_____

HOW OFTEN DID YOU FILL OUT THIS CHART

NOT AT ALL [ ]   1-3X PER WEEK [ ]   ALMOST EVERY DAY [ ]   EVERYDAY [ ]

MEDICATION & SUPPLEMENT TRACKER

MEDICATION NAME	DOSE.	MON	TUES	WED	THURS	FRI	SAT	SUN
EXAMPLE	5mg							

_____

_____

_____

_____

_____

_____

_____

_____

WHAT GOALS DO YOU HAVE FOR YOUR HEALTH?

ANSWER THESE QUESTIONS TO BREAK OUT OF NEGATIVE THOUGHT PATTERNS AND REFOCUS ON THE THINGS THAT MAKE YOU HAPPY AND GRATEFUL.

DAILY ENERGY vs MOOD TRACKER

TRACK YOUR DAILY ENERGY, MOOD AND ALSO PAIN USING DIFFERENT COLOURS ON THIS LINE CHART

100

75

50

25

0

ENERGY

| MONDAY | TUESDAY | WEDNESDAY | THURSDAY | FRIDAY | SATURDAY | SUNDAY |

PAIN

TIME OF DAY PAIN TRACKER

MORNING

0 1 2 3 4 5 6 7 8 9 10

No Pain   Moderate Pain   Worst Pain

AFTERNOON

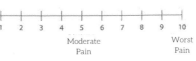

0 1 2 3 4 5 6 7 8 9 10

No Pain   Moderate Pain   Worst Pain

EVENING

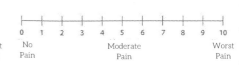

0 1 2 3 4 5 6 7 8 9 10

No Pain   Moderate Pain   Worst Pain

MORNING

0 1 2 3 4 5 6 7 8 9 10

No Pain   Moderate Pain   Worst Pain

AFTERNOON

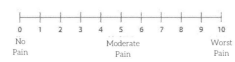

0 1 2 3 4 5 6 7 8 9 10

No Pain   Moderate Pain   Worst Pain

EVENING

0 1 2 3 4 5 6 7 8 9 10

No Pain   Moderate Pain   Worst Pain

MORNING

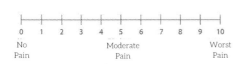

0 1 2 3 4 5 6 7 8 9 10

No Pain   Moderate Pain   Worst Pain

AFTERNOON

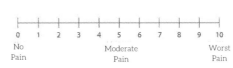

0 1 2 3 4 5 6 7 8 9 10

No Pain   Moderate Pain   Worst Pain

EVENING

0 1 2 3 4 5 6 7 8 9 10

No Pain   Moderate Pain   Worst Pain

MORNING

0 1 2 3 4 5 6 7 8 9 10

No Pain   Moderate Pain   Worst Pain

AFTERNOON

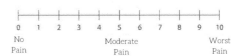

0 1 2 3 4 5 6 7 8 9 10

No Pain   Moderate Pain   Worst Pain

EVENING

0 1 2 3 4 5 6 7 8 9 10

No Pain   Moderate Pain   Worst Pain

MORNING

0 1 2 3 4 5 6 7 8 9 10

No Pain   Moderate Pain   Worst Pain

AFTERNOON

0 1 2 3 4 5 6 7 8 9 10

No Pain   Moderate Pain   Worst Pain

EVENING

0 1 2 3 4 5 6 7 8 9 10

No Pain   Moderate Pain   Worst Pain

SYMPTOM & TRIGGER TRACKER

	FREQ. / SEVERITY Y/N	MON	TUES	WED	THURS	FRI	SAT	SUN
DID YOU HAVE A GOOD DAY? (YES NO, 0-5 BAD TO GOOD)	Y/N 0-5	☐	☐	☐	☐	☐	☐	☐
MUSCLE PAIN OR WEAKNESS	0-5							
JOINT PAIN	0-5							
ENERGY LEVELS	0-5							
ANXIETY	0-5							
DIFFICULTY SLEEPING	0-5							
FEELING DEPRESSED / LOW MOOD	0-5							
OVER SLEEPING	Y/N							
DROWSIENESS	0-5							
HEADACHE / MIGRAINE	Y/N							
NAUSEA	0-5							
DIARRHOEA	0-5							
CONSTIPATION	Y-N							
BLOATING	0-5							
ACID REFLUX	Y/N							
NUMBNESS OR TINGLING	0-5							
HAIR LOSS	0-5							
SWOLLEN LYMPH NODES	0-5							
HEART PALPITATIONS	Y/N							
DRY EYES OR VISION PROBLEMS	0-5							
RINGING IN EARS	Y/N							
SENSITIVITY TO LIGHT	0-5							
SENSITIVITY TO SOUND	Y/N							
FACIAL NUMBNESS	Y/N							
BRAIN FOG / DIFFICULTY CONCENTRATING	Y/N							
HEADACHE OR MIGRAINE	Y/N							

CONTINUE TO THE NEXT PAGE

SYMPTOM & TRIGGER TRACKER

	FREQ. / SEVERITY Y/N	MON	TUES	WED	THURS	FRI	SAT	SUN
EXERCISE	MINS							
RASH	0-5							
MOUTH SORES	Y/N							
SKIN RASH	0-5							
UTI, DARK URINE OR OTHER BLADDER ISSUES	0-5							
LOW GRADE FEVER	TEMP							
COLD OR INFECTION	Y/N							
SHORTNESS OF BREATH	Y/N							
MEDICATION:	DOSE	☐	☐	☐	☐	☐	☐	☐
MEDICATION:	DOSE							
MEDICATION:	DOSE							
MEDICATION:	DOSE							

FILL IN THE CHARTS TO TRACK SYMPTOMS AND THEN PUT DETAILS AND POST POSSIBLE TRIGGERS IN THE NOTES BELOW.

_____
_____
_____
_____
_____
_____
_____
_____
_____
_____
_____
_____

HOW OFTEN DID YOU FILL OUT THIS CHART

NOT AT ALL   [ ]   1-3X PER WEEK   [ ]   ALMOST EVERY DAY   [ ]   EVERYDAY   [ ]

SYMPTOM TRACKER

DATE	TIME	DURATION	DESCRIPTION
DATE	TIME	DURATION	DESCRIPTION

TIME OF DAY SYMPTOM TRACKER

TRACK THE SEVERITY OF YOUR SYMPTOMS THROUGHOUT THE DAY USING THE
SCALE, USE THE NOTE SECTION BELOW TO LIST THE SYMPTOMS YOU EXPERIENCED.
USE THIS TO SEE IF CERTAIN TIMES OF DAY E.G. MEAL TIMES OR FIRST THING IN THE
MORNING, ARE TRIGGERS FOR YOU.

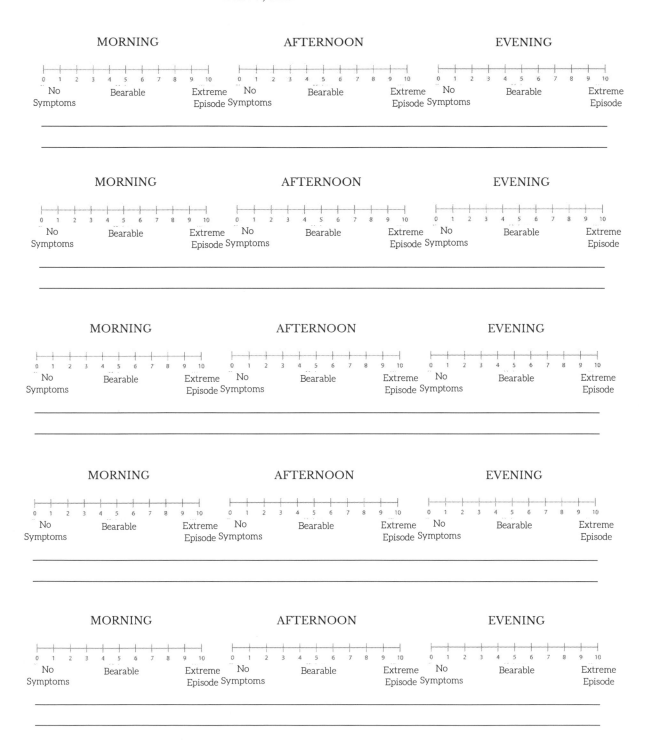

PAIN TRACKER BAR CHART

1

2

3

4

5

6

7

8

9

10

MONDAY	TUESDAY	WEDNESDAY	THURSDAY	FRIDAY	SATURDAY	SUNDAY

FOOD LOG AND FOOD TRIGGER TRACKER

FOOD	AMOUNT	TIME	IMMEDIATELY AFTER	1 HOUR	3 HOURS

LOG HOW YOU FEEL AFTER FOOD IN THESE SECTIONS

FOOD TRACKER

MEAL	MONDAY	TUESDAY	WEDNESDAY	THURSDAY	FRIDAY	SATURDAY	SUNDAY
BREAKFAST							
LUNCH							
DINNER							
CALORIES (OPTIONAL)							
SUPPLEMENTS	MULTIVIT [ ] VITAMIN D [ ] CALCIUM [ ]	MULTIVIT [ ] VITAMIN D [ ] CALCIUM [ ]	MULTIVIT [ ] VITAMIN D [ ] CALCIUM [ ]	MULTIVIT [ ] VITAMIN D [ ] CALCIUM [ ]	MULTIVIT [ ] VITAMIN D [ ] CALCIUM [ ]	MULTIVIT [ ] VITAMIN D [ ] CALCIUM [ ]	MULTIVIT [ ] VITAMIN D [ ] CALCIUM [ ]
WATER INTAKE							

EXERCISE	MONDAY	TUESDAY	WEDNESDAY	THURSDAY	FRIDAY	SATURDAY	SUNDAY

FILL IN THE NOTES BELOW ON AREAS FOR IMPROVEMENT, SHOPPING LISTS, HOW YOU FELT AFTER YOU ATE, CALORIES, SNACKS AND WHATEVER YOU THINK WOULD BE USEFUL TO ADD TO YOUR FOOD JOURNAL

_____

_____

_____

_____

_____

_____

_____

_____

_____

_____

HOW OFTEN DID YOU FILL OUT THIS CHART

NOT AT ALL   [ ]   1-3X PER WEEK   [ ]   ALMOST EVERY DAY   [ ]   EVERYDAY   [ ]

MEDICATION & SUPPLEMENT TRACKER

MEDICATION NAME	DOSE.	MON	TUES	WED	THURS	FRI	SAT	SUN
EXAMPLE	5mg							

_____

_____

_____

_____

_____

_____

_____

_____

WHO ARE YOU MOST GRATEFUL FOR?

ANSWER THESE QUESTIONS TO BREAK OUT OF NEGATIVE
THOUGHT PATTERNS AND REFOCUS ON THE THINGS THAT MAKE
YOU HAPPY AND GRATEFUL.

DAILY ENERGY vs MOOD TRACKER

TRACK YOUR DAILY ENERGY, MOOD AND ALSO PAIN USING DIFFERENT COLOURS ON THIS LINE CHART

100

75

50

25

0   MONDAY   TUESDAY   WEDNESDAY   THURSDAY   FRIDAY   SATURDAY   SUNDAY

ENERGY

PAIN

TIME OF DAY PAIN TRACKER

MORNING

0 1 2 3 4 5 6 7 8 9 10
No Pain   Moderate Pain   Worst Pain

AFTERNOON

0 1 2 3 4 5 6 7 8 9 10
No Pain   Moderate Pain   Worst Pain

EVENING

0 1 2 3 4 5 6 7 8 9 10
No Pain   Moderate Pain   Worst Pain

MORNING

0 1 2 3 4 5 6 7 8 9 10
No Pain   Moderate Pain   Worst Pain

AFTERNOON

0 1 2 3 4 5 6 7 8 9 10
No Pain   Moderate Pain   Worst Pain

EVENING

0 1 2 3 4 5 6 7 8 9 10
No Pain   Moderate Pain   Worst Pain

MORNING

0 1 2 3 4 5 6 7 8 9 10
No Pain   Moderate Pain   Worst Pain

AFTERNOON

0 1 2 3 4 5 6 7 8 9 10
No Pain   Moderate Pain   Worst Pain

EVENING

0 1 2 3 4 5 6 7 8 9 10
No Pain   Moderate Pain   Worst Pain

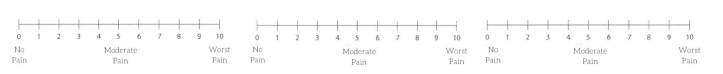

MORNING

0 1 2 3 4 5 6 7 8 9 10
No Pain   Moderate Pain   Worst Pain

AFTERNOON

0 1 2 3 4 5 6 7 8 9 10
No Pain   Moderate Pain   Worst Pain

EVENING

0 1 2 3 4 5 6 7 8 9 10
No Pain   Moderate Pain   Worst Pain

MORNING

0 1 2 3 4 5 6 7 8 9 10
No Pain   Moderate Pain   Worst Pain

AFTERNOON

0 1 2 3 4 5 6 7 8 9 10
No Pain   Moderate Pain   Worst Pain

EVENING

0 1 2 3 4 5 6 7 8 9 10
No Pain   Moderate Pain   Worst Pain

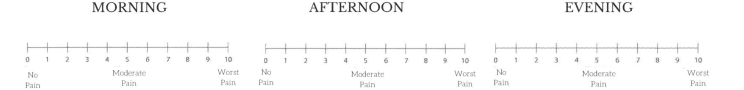

SYMPTOM & TRIGGER TRACKER

	FREQ. / SEVERITY Y/N	MON	TUES	WED	THURS	FRI	SAT	SUN
DID YOU HAVE A GOOD DAY? (YES NO, 0-5 BAD TO GOOD)	Y/N 0-5	☐	☐	☐	☐	☐	☐	☐
MUSCLE PAIN OR WEAKNESS	0-5							
JOINT PAIN	0-5							
ENERGY LEVELS	0-5							
ANXIETY	0-5							
DIFFICULTY SLEEPING	0-5							
FEELING DEPRESSED / LOW MOOD	0-5							
OVER SLEEPING	Y/N							
DROWSIENESS	0-5							
HEADACHE / MIGRAINE	Y/N							
NAUSEA	0-5							
DIARRHOEA	0-5							
CONSTIPATION	Y-N							
BLOATING	0-5							
ACID REFLUX	Y/N							
NUMBNESS OR TINGLING	0-5							
HAIR LOSS	0-5							
SWOLLEN LYMPH NODES	0-5							
HEART PALPITATIONS	Y/N							
DRY EYES OR VISION PROBLEMS	0-5							
RINGING IN EARS	Y/N							
SENSITIVITY TO LIGHT	0-5							
SENSITIVITY TO SOUND	Y/N							
FACIAL NUMBNESS	Y/N							
BRAIN FOG / DIFFICULTY CONCENTRATING	Y/N							
HEADACHE OR MIGRAINE	Y/N							

CONTINUE TO THE NEXT PAGE

SYMPTOM & TRIGGER TRACKER

	FREQ. / SEVERITY Y/N	MON	TUES	WED	THURS	FRI	SAT	SUN
EXERCISE	MINS							
RASH	0-5							
MOUTH SORES	Y/N							
SKIN RASH	0-5							
UTI, DARK URINE OR OTHER BLADDER ISSUES	0-5							
LOW GRADE FEVER	TEMP							
COLD OR INFECTION	Y/N							
SHORTNESS OF BREATH	Y/N							
MEDICATION:	DOSE							
MEDICATION:	DOSE							
MEDICATION:	DOSE							
MEDICATION:	DOSE							

FILL IN THE CHARTS TO TRACK SYMPTOMS AND THEN PUT DETAILS AND POST POSSIBLE TRIGGERS IN THE NOTES BELOW.

_____
_____
_____
_____
_____
_____
_____
_____
_____
_____
_____
_____
_____
_____

HOW OFTEN DID YOU FILL OUT THIS CHART

NOT AT ALL   [ ]   1-3X PER WEEK   [ ]   ALMOST EVERY DAY   [ ]   EVERYDAY   [ ]

SYMPTOM TRACKER

DATE	TIME	DURATION	DESCRIPTION
DATE	TIME	DURATION	DESCRIPTION

TIME OF DAY SYMPTOM TRACKER

TRACK THE SEVERITY OF YOUR SYMPTOMS THROUGHOUT THE DAY USING THE
SCALE, USE THE NOTE SECTION BELOW TO LIST THE SYMPTOMS YOU EXPERIENCED.
USE THIS TO SEE IF CERTAIN TIMES OF DAY E.G. MEAL TIMES OR FIRST THING IN THE
MORNING, ARE TRIGGERS FOR YOU.

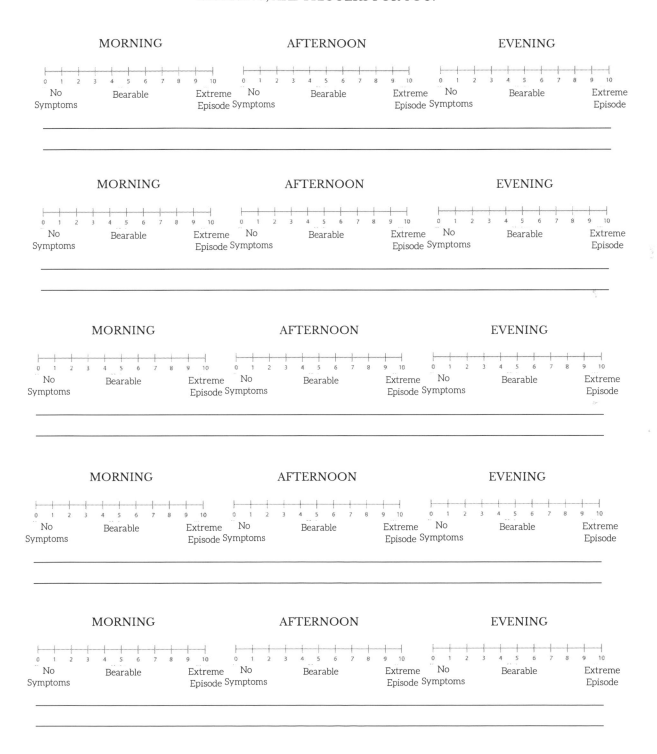

PAIN TRACKER BAR CHART

1

2

3

4

5

6

7

8

9

10

| MONDAY | TUESDAY | WEDNESDAY | THURSDAY | FRIDAY | SATURDAY | SUNDAY |

FOOD LOG AND FOOD TRIGGER TRACKER

FOOD	AMOUNT	TIME	IMMEDIATELY AFTER	1 HOUR	3 HOURS

LOG HOW YOU FEEL AFTER FOOD IN THESE SECTIONS

FOOD TRACKER

MEAL	MONDAY	TUESDAY	WEDNESDAY	THURSDAY	FRIDAY	SATURDAY	SUNDAY
BREAKFAST							
LUNCH							
DINNER							
CALORIES (OPTIONAL)							
SUPPLEMENTS	MULTIVIT ☐ VITAMIN D ☐ CALCIUM ☐	MULTIVIT ☐ VITAMIN D ☐ CALCIUM ☐	MULTIVIT ☐ VITAMIN D ☐ CALCIUM ☐	MULTIVIT ☐ VITAMIN D ☐ CALCIUM ☐	MULTIVIT ☐ VITAMIN D ☐ CALCIUM ☐	MULTIVIT ☐ VITAMIN D ☐ CALCIUM ☐	MULTIVIT ☐ VITAMIN D ☐ CALCIUM ☐
WATER INTAKE	☐☐☐ ☐☐☐	☐☐☐☐ ☐☐☐☐	☐☐☐☐ ☐☐☐☐	☐☐☐☐ ☐☐☐☐	☐☐☐☐ ☐☐☐☐	☐☐☐☐ ☐☐☐☐	☐☐☐☐ ☐☐☐☐

EXERCISE	MONDAY	TUESDAY	WEDNESDAY	THURSDAY	FRIDAY	SATURDAY	SUNDAY

FILL IN THE NOTES BELOW ON AREAS FOR IMPROVEMENT, SHOPPING LISTS, HOW YOU FELT AFTER YOU ATE, CALORIES, SNACKS AND WHATEVER YOU THINK WOULD BE USEFUL TO ADD TO YOUR FOOD JOURNAL

_____

_____

_____

_____

_____

_____

_____

_____

_____

HOW OFTEN DID YOU FILL OUT THIS CHART

NOT AT ALL   [ ]   1-3X PER WEEK   [ ]   ALMOST EVERY DAY   [ ]   EVERYDAY   [ ]

MEDICATION & SUPPLEMENT TRACKER

MEDICATION NAME	DOSE.	MON	TUES	WED	THURS	FRI	SAT	SUN
EXAMPLE	5mg							

_____

_____

_____

_____

_____

_____

_____

_____

WHEN IS GRATITUDE IMPORTANT?

ANSWER THESE QUESTIONS TO BREAK OUT OF NEGATIVE
THOUGHT PATTERNS AND REFOCUS ON THE THINGS THAT MAKE
YOU HAPPY AND GRATEFUL.

DAILY ENERGY vs MOOD TRACKER

TRACK YOUR DAILY ENERGY, MOOD AND ALSO PAIN USING DIFFERENT COLOURS ON THIS LINE CHART

100

75

50

25

0

MONDAY   TUESDAY   WEDNESDAY   THURSDAY   FRIDAY   SATURDAY   SUNDAY

ENERGY

PAIN

TIME OF DAY PAIN TRACKER

MORNING

0 1 2 3 4 5 6 7 8 9 10
No Pain   Moderate Pain   Worst Pain

AFTERNOON

0 1 2 3 4 5 6 7 8 9 10
No Pain   Moderate Pain   Worst Pain

EVENING

0 1 2 3 4 5 6 7 8 9 10
No Pain   Moderate Pain   Worst Pain

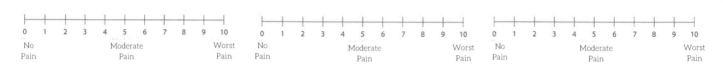

MORNING

0 1 2 3 4 5 6 7 8 9 10
No Pain   Moderate Pain   Worst Pain

AFTERNOON

0 1 2 3 4 5 6 7 8 9 10
No Pain   Moderate Pain   Worst Pain

EVENING

0 1 2 3 4 5 6 7 8 9 10
No Pain   Moderate Pain   Worst Pain

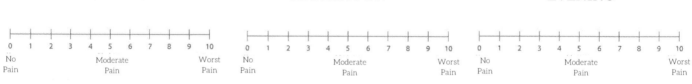

MORNING

0 1 2 3 4 5 6 7 8 9 10
No Pain   Moderate Pain   Worst Pain

AFTERNOON

0 1 2 3 4 5 6 7 8 9 10
No Pain   Moderate Pain   Worst Pain

EVENING

0 1 2 3 4 5 6 7 8 9 10
No Pain   Moderate Pain   Worst Pain

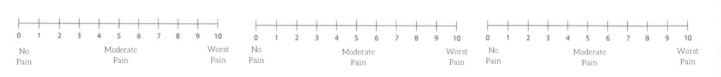

MORNING

0 1 2 3 4 5 6 7 8 9 10
No Pain   Moderate Pain   Worst Pain

AFTERNOON

0 1 2 3 4 5 6 7 8 9 10
No Pain   Moderate Pain   Worst Pain

EVENING

0 1 2 3 4 5 6 7 8 9 10
No Pain   Moderate Pain   Worst Pain

MORNING

0 1 2 3 4 5 6 7 8 9 10
No Pain   Moderate Pain   Worst Pain

AFTERNOON

0 1 2 3 4 5 6 7 8 9 10
No Pain   Moderate Pain   Worst Pain

EVENING

0 1 2 3 4 5 6 7 8 9 10
No Pain   Moderate Pain   Worst Pain

SYMPTOM & TRIGGER TRACKER

	FREQ. / SEVERITY Y/N	MON	TUES	WED	THURS	FRI	SAT	SUN
DID YOU HAVE A GOOD DAY? (YES NO, 0-5 BAD TO GOOD)	Y/N 0-5	☐	☐	☐	☐	☐	☐	☐
MUSCLE PAIN OR WEAKNESS	0-5							
JOINT PAIN	0-5							
ENERGY LEVELS	0-5							
ANXIETY	0-5							
DIFFICULTY SLEEPING	0-5							
FEELING DEPRESSED / LOW MOOD	0-5							
OVER SLEEPING	Y/N							
DROWSIENESS	0-5							
HEADACHE / MIGRAINE	Y/N							
NAUSEA	0-5							
DIARRHOEA	0-5							
CONSTIPATION	Y-N							
BLOATING	0-5							
ACID REFLUX	Y/N							
NUMBNESS OR TINGLING	0-5							
HAIR LOSS	0-5							
SWOLLEN LYMPH NODES	0-5							
HEART PALPITATIONS	Y/N							
DRY EYES OR VISION PROBLEMS	0-5							
RINGING IN EARS	Y/N							
SENSITIVITY TO LIGHT	0-5							
SENSITIVITY TO SOUND	Y/N							
FACIAL NUMBNESS	Y/N							
BRAIN FOG / DIFFICULTY CONCENTRATING	Y/N							
HEADACHE OR MIGRAINE	Y/N							

CONTINUE TO THE NEXT PAGE

SYMPTOM & TRIGGER TRACKER

	FREQ. / SEVERITY Y/N	MON	TUES	WED	THURS	FRI	SAT	SUN
EXERCISE	MINS							
RASH	0-5							
MOUTH SORES	Y/N							
SKIN RASH	0-5							
UTI, DARK URINE OR OTHER BLADDER ISSUES	0-5							
LOW GRADE FEVER	TEMP							
COLD OR INFECTION	Y/N							
SHORTNESS OF BREATH	Y/N							
MEDICATION:	DOSE	☐	☐	☐	☐	☐	☐	☐
MEDICATION:	DOSE							
MEDICATION:	DOSE							
MEDICATION:	DOSE							

FILL IN THE CHARTS TO TRACK SYMPTOMS AND THEN PUT DETAILS AND POST POSSIBLE TRIGGERS IN THE NOTES BELOW.

_____
_____
_____
_____
_____
_____
_____
_____
_____
_____
_____
_____
_____
_____

HOW OFTEN DID YOU FILL OUT THIS CHART

NOT AT ALL   [ ]   1-3X PER WEEK   [ ]   ALMOST EVERY DAY   [ ]   EVERYDAY   [ ]

SYMPTOM TRACKER

DATE	TIME	DURATION	DESCRIPTION
DATE	TIME	DURATION	DESCRIPTION

TIME OF DAY SYMPTOM TRACKER

TRACK THE SEVERITY OF YOUR SYMPTOMS THROUGHOUT THE DAY USING THE SCALE, USE THE NOTE SECTION BELOW TO LIST THE SYMPTOMS YOU EXPERIENCED. USE THIS TO SEE IF CERTAIN TIMES OF DAY E.G. MEAL TIMES OR FIRST THING IN THE MORNING, ARE TRIGGERS FOR YOU.

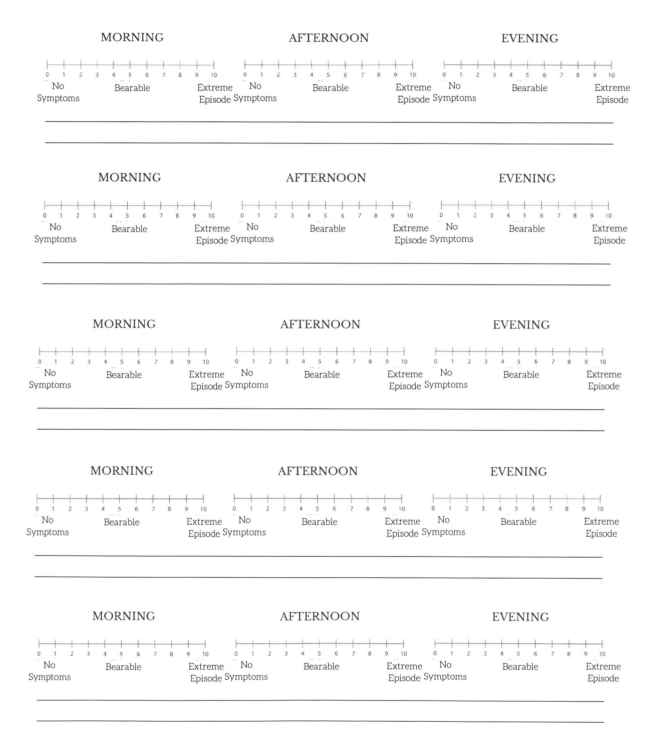

PAIN TRACKER BAR CHART

1

2

3

4

5

6

7

8

9

10

| MONDAY | TUESDAY | WEDNESDAY | THURSDAY | FRIDAY | SATURDAY | SUNDAY |

FOOD LOG AND FOOD TRIGGER TRACKER

FOOD	AMOUNT	TIME	IMMEDIATELY AFTER	1 HOUR	3 HOURS

LOG HOW YOU FEEL AFTER FOOD IN THESE SECTIONS

FOOD TRACKER

MEAL	MONDAY	TUESDAY	WEDNESDAY	THURSDAY	FRIDAY	SATURDAY	SUNDAY
BREAKFAST							
LUNCH							
DINNER							
CALORIES (OPTIONAL)							
SUPPLEMENTS	MULTIVIT ☐	MULTIVIT ☐	MULTIVIT ☐	MULTIVIT ☐	MULTIVIT ☐	MULTIVIT ☐	MULTIVIT ☐
	VITAMIN D ☐	VITAMIN D ☐	VITAMIN D ☐	VITAMIN D ☐	VITAMIN D ☐	VITAMIN D ☐	VITAMIN D ☐
	CALCIUM ☐	CALCIUM ☐	CALCIUM ☐	CALCIUM ☐	CALCIUM ☐	CALCIUM ☐	CALCIUM ☐
WATER INTAKE	☐☐☐	☐☐☐	☐☐☐	☐☐☐	☐☐☐	☐☐☐	☐☐☐

EXERCISE	MONDAY	TUESDAY	WEDNESDAY	THURSDAY	FRIDAY	SATURDAY	SUNDAY

FILL IN THE NOTES BELOW ON AREAS FOR IMPROVEMENT, SHOPPING LISTS, HOW YOU FELT AFTER YOU ATE, CALORIES, SNACKS AND WHATEVER YOU THINK WOULD BE USEFUL TO ADD TO YOUR FOOD JOURNAL

_____

_____

_____

_____

_____

_____

_____

_____

_____

_____

HOW OFTEN DID YOU FILL OUT THIS CHART

NOT AT ALL   [ ]   1-3X PER WEEK   [ ]   ALMOST EVERY DAY   [ ]   EVERYDAY   [ ]

MEDICATION & SUPPLEMENT TRACKER

MEDICATION NAME	DOSE.	MON	TUES	WED	THURS	FRI	SAT	SUN
EXAMPLE	5mg							

_____

_____

_____

_____

_____

_____

_____

_____

WHAT HAVE YOU SEEN TODAY YOU ARE THANKFUL FOR?

ANSWER THESE QUESTIONS TO BREAK OUT OF NEGATIVE
THOUGHT PATTERNS AND REFOCUS ON THE THINGS THAT MAKE
YOU HAPPY AND GRATEFUL.

DAILY ENERGY vs MOOD TRACKER

TRACK YOUR DAILY ENERGY, MOOD AND ALSO PAIN USING DIFFERENT COLOURS ON THIS LINE CHART

100

75

50

25

0   MONDAY   TUESDAY   WEDNESDAY   THURSDAY   FRIDAY   SATURDAY   SUNDAY

ENERGY

PAIN

TIME OF DAY PAIN TRACKER

MORNING

| | | | | | | | | | | |
|0|1|2|3|4|5|6|7|8|9|10|

No Pain   Moderate Pain   Worst Pain

AFTERNOON

| | | | | | | | | | | |
|0|1|2|3|4|5|6|7|8|9|10|

No Pain   Moderate Pain   Worst Pain

EVENING

| | | | | | | | | | | |
|0|1|2|3|4|5|6|7|8|9|10|

No Pain   Moderate Pain   Worst Pain

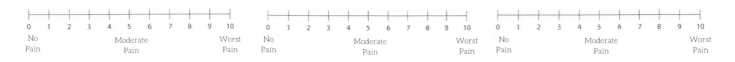

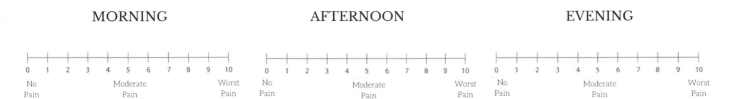

MORNING   AFTERNOON   EVENING

0 1 2 3 4 5 6 7 8 9 10

No Pain — Moderate Pain — Worst Pain

MORNING   AFTERNOON   EVENING

0 1 2 3 4 5 6 7 8 9 10

No Pain — Moderate Pain — Worst Pain

MORNING   AFTERNOON   EVENING

0 1 2 3 4 5 6 7 8 9 10

No Pain — Moderate Pain — Worst Pain

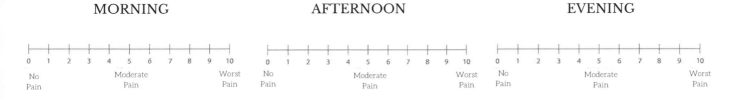

MORNING   AFTERNOON   EVENING

0 1 2 3 4 5 6 7 8 9 10

No Pain — Moderate Pain — Worst Pain

SYMPTOM & TRIGGER TRACKER

	FREQ. / SEVERITY Y/N	MON	TUES	WED	THURS	FRI	SAT	SUN
DID YOU HAVE A GOOD DAY? (YES NO, 0-5 BAD TO GOOD)	Y/N 0-5	☐	☐	☐	☐	☐	☐	☐
MUSCLE PAIN OR WEAKNESS	0-5							
JOINT PAIN	0-5							
ENERGY LEVELS	0-5							
ANXIETY	0-5							
DIFFICULTY SLEEPING	0-5							
FEELING DEPRESSED / LOW MOOD	0-5							
OVER SLEEPING	Y/N							
DROWSIENESS	0-5							
HEADACHE / MIGRAINE	Y/N							
NAUSEA	0-5							
DIARRHOEA	0-5							
CONSTIPATION	Y-N							
BLOATING	0-5							
ACID REFLUX	Y/N							
NUMBNESS OR TINGLING	0-5							
HAIR LOSS	0-5							
SWOLLEN LYMPH NODES	0-5							
HEART PALPITATIONS	Y/N							
DRY EYES OR VISION PROBLEMS	0-5							
RINGING IN EAR'S	Y/N							
SENSITIVITY TO LIGHT	0-5							
SENSITIVITY TO SOUND	Y/N							
FACIAL NUMBNESS	Y/N							
BRAIN FOG / DIFFICULTY CONCENTRATING	Y/N							
HEADACHE OR MIGRAINE	Y/N							

CONTINUE TO THE NEXT PAGE

SYMPTOM & TRIGGER TRACKER

	FREQ. / SEVERITY Y/N	MON	TUES	WED	THURS	FRI	SAT	SUN
EXERCISE	MINS							
RASH	0-5							
MOUTH SORES	Y/N							
SKIN RASH	0-5							
UTI, DARK URINE OR OTHER BLADDER ISSUES	0-5							
LOW GRADE FEVER	TEMP							
COLD OR INFECTION	Y/N							
SHORTNESS OF BREATH	Y/N							
MEDICATION:	DOSE	☐	☐	☐	☐	☐	☐	☐
MEDICATION:	DOSE							
MEDICATION:	DOSE							
MEDICATION:	DOSE							

FILL IN THE CHARTS TO TRACK SYMPTOMS AND THEN PUT DETAILS AND POST POSSIBLE TRIGGERS IN THE NOTES BELOW.

_____

_____

_____

_____

_____

_____

_____

_____

_____

_____

_____

_____

HOW OFTEN DID YOU FILL OUT THIS CHART

NOT AT ALL   [ ]   1-3X PER WEEK   [ ]   ALMOST EVERY DAY   [ ]   EVERYDAY   [ ]

SYMPTOM TRACKER

DATE	TIME	DURATION	DESCRIPTION

TIME OF DAY SYMPTOM TRACKER

TRACK THE SEVERITY OF YOUR SYMPTOMS THROUGHOUT THE DAY USING THE
SCALE, USE THE NOTE SECTION BELOW TO LIST THE SYMPTOMS YOU EXPERIENCED.
USE THIS TO SEE IF CERTAIN TIMES OF DAY E.G. MEAL TIMES OR FIRST THING IN THE
MORNING, ARE TRIGGERS FOR YOU.

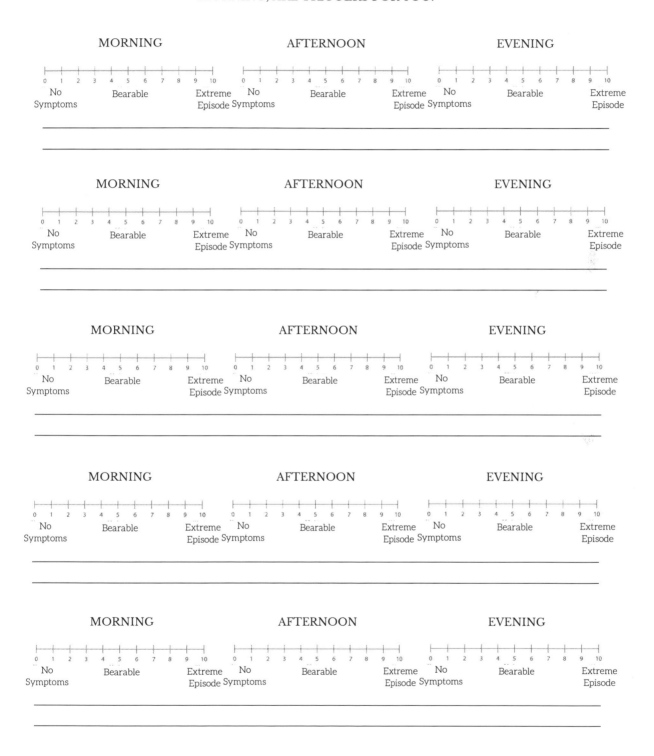

PAIN TRACKER BAR CHART

1

2

3

4

5

6

7

8

9

10

| MONDAY | TUESDAY | WEDNESDAY | THURSDAY | FRIDAY | SATURDAY | SUNDAY |

FOOD LOG AND FOOD TRIGGER TRACKER

FOOD	AMOUNT	TIME	IMMEDIATELY AFTER	1 HOUR	3 HOURS

LOG HOW YOU FEEL AFTER FOOD IN THESE SECTIONS

FOOD TRACKER

MEAL	MONDAY	TUESDAY	WEDNESDAY	THURSDAY	FRIDAY	SATURDAY	SUNDAY
BREAKFAST							
LUNCH							
DINNER							
CALORIES (OPTIONAL)							
SUPPLEMENTS	MULTIVIT [ ] VITAMIN D [ ] CALCIUM [ ]	MULTIVIT [ ] VITAMIN D [ ] CALCIUM [ ]	MULTIVIT [ ] VITAMIN D [ ] CALCIUM [ ]	MULTIVIT [ ] VITAMIN D [ ] CALCIUM [ ]	MULTIVIT [ ] VITAMIN D [ ] CALCIUM [ ]	MULTIVIT [ ] VITAMIN D [ ] CALCIUM [ ]	MULTIVIT [ ] VITAMIN D [ ] CALCIUM [ ]
WATER INTAKE							

EXERCISE	MONDAY	TUESDAY	WEDNESDAY	THURSDAY	FRIDAY	SATURDAY	SUNDAY

FILL IN THE NOTES BELOW ON AREAS FOR IMPROVEMENT, SHOPPING LISTS, HOW YOU FELT AFTER YOU ATE, CALORIES, SNACKS AND WHATEVER YOU THINK WOULD BE USEFUL TO ADD TO YOUR FOOD JOURNAL

_____

_____

_____

_____

_____

_____

_____

_____

_____

HOW OFTEN DID YOU FILL OUT THIS CHART

NOT AT ALL   [ ]   1-3X PER WEEK   [ ]   ALMOST EVERY DAY   [ ]   EVERYDAY   [ ]

MEDICATION & SUPPLEMENT TRACKER

MEDICATION NAME	DOSE.	MON	TUES	WED	THURS	FRI	SAT	SUN
EXAMPLE	5mg							

_____

_____

_____

_____

_____

_____

_____

WHAT BODY PART ARE YOU GRATEFUL FOR?

ANSWER THESE QUESTIONS TO BREAK OUT OF NEGATIVE
THOUGHT PATTERNS AND REFOCUS ON THE THINGS THAT MAKE
YOU HAPPY AND GRATEFUL.

DAILY ENERGY vs MOOD TRACKER

TRACK YOUR DAILY ENERGY, MOOD AND ALSO PAIN USING DIFFERENT COLOURS ON THIS LINE CHART

100

75

50

25

0

MONDAY	TUESDAY	WEDNESDAY	THURSDAY	FRIDAY	SATURDAY	SUNDAY

ENERGY

PAIN

TIME OF DAY PAIN TRACKER

MORNING   AFTERNOON   EVENING

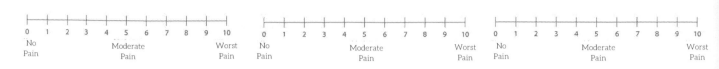

0 1 2 3 4 5 6 7 8 9 10
No Pain   Moderate Pain   Worst Pain

MORNING   AFTERNOON   EVENING

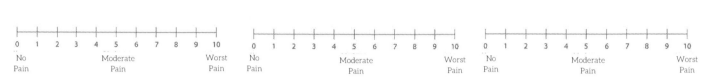

0 1 2 3 4 5 6 7 8 9 10
No Pain   Moderate Pain   Worst Pain

MORNING   AFTERNOON   EVENING

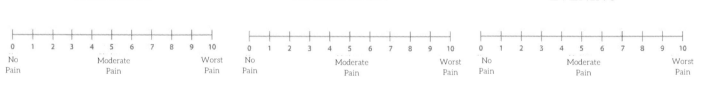

0 1 2 3 4 5 6 7 8 9 10
No Pain   Moderate Pain   Worst Pain

MORNING   AFTERNOON   EVENING

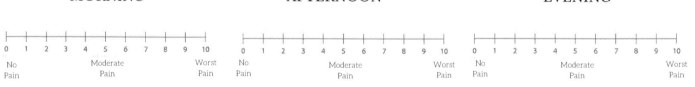

0 1 2 3 4 5 6 7 8 9 10
No Pain   Moderate Pain   Worst Pain

MORNING   AFTERNOON   EVENING

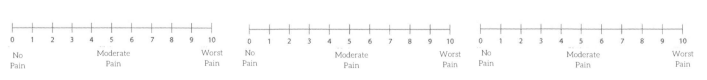

0 1 2 3 4 5 6 7 8 9 10
No Pain   Moderate Pain   Worst Pain

SYMPTOM & TRIGGER TRACKER

	FREQ. / SEVERITY Y/N	MON	TUES	WED	THURS	FRI	SAT	SUN
DID YOU HAVE A GOOD DAY? (YES NO, 0-5 BAD TO GOOD)	Y/N 0-5	☐	☐	☐	☐	☐	☐	☐
MUSCLE PAIN OR WEAKNESS	0-5							
JOINT PAIN	0-5							
ENERGY LEVELS	0-5							
ANXIETY	0-5							
DIFFICULTY SLEEPING	0-5							
FEELING DEPRESSED / LOW MOOD	0-5							
OVER SLEEPING	Y/N							
DROWSIENESS	0-5							
HEADACHE / MIGRAINE	Y/N							
NAUSEA	0-5							
DIARRHOEA	0-5							
CONSTIPATION	Y-N							
BLOATING	0-5							
ACID REFLUX	Y/N							
NUMBNESS OR TINGLING	0-5							
HAIR LOSS	0-5							
SWOLLEN LYMPH NODES	0-5							
HEART PALPITATIONS	Y/N							
DRY EYES OR VISION PROBLEMS	0-5							
RINGING IN EARS	Y/N							
SENSITIVITY TO LIGHT	0-5							
SENSITIVITY TO SOUND	Y/N							
FACIAL NUMBNESS	Y/N							
BRAIN FOG / DIFFICULTY CONCENTRATING	Y/N							
HEADACHE OR MIGRAINE	Y/N							

CONTINUE TO THE NEXT PAGE

SYMPTOM & TRIGGER TRACKER

	FREQ. / SEVERITY Y/N	MON	TUES	WED	THURS	FRI	SAT	SUN
EXERCISE	MINS							
RASH	0-5							
MOUTH SORES	Y/N							
SKIN RASH	0-5							
UTI, DARK URINE OR OTHER BLADDER ISSUES	0-5							
LOW GRADE FEVER	TEMP							
COLD OR INFECTION	Y/N							
SHORTNESS OF BREATH	Y/N							
MEDICATION:	DOSE	☐	☐	☐	☐	☐	☐	☐
MEDICATION:	DOSE							
MEDICATION:	DOSE							
MEDICATION:	DOSE							

FILL IN THE CHARTS TO TRACK SYMPTOMS AND THEN PUT DETAILS AND POST POSSIBLE TRIGGERS IN THE NOTES BELOW.

_____
_____
_____
_____
_____
_____
_____
_____
_____
_____
_____
_____
_____

HOW OFTEN DID YOU FILL OUT THIS CHART
NOT AT ALL   [ ]   1-3X PER WEEK   [ ]   ALMOST EVERY DAY   [ ]   EVERYDAY   [ ]

SYMPTOM TRACKER

DATE	TIME	DURATION	DESCRIPTION
DATE	TIME	DURATION	DESCRIPTION

TIME OF DAY SYMPTOM TRACKER

TRACK THE SEVERITY OF YOUR SYMPTOMS THROUGHOUT THE DAY USING THE SCALE, USE THE NOTE SECTION BELOW TO LIST THE SYMPTOMS YOU EXPERIENCED. USE THIS TO SEE IF CERTAIN TIMES OF DAY E.G. MEAL TIMES OR FIRST THING IN THE MORNING, ARE TRIGGERS FOR YOU.

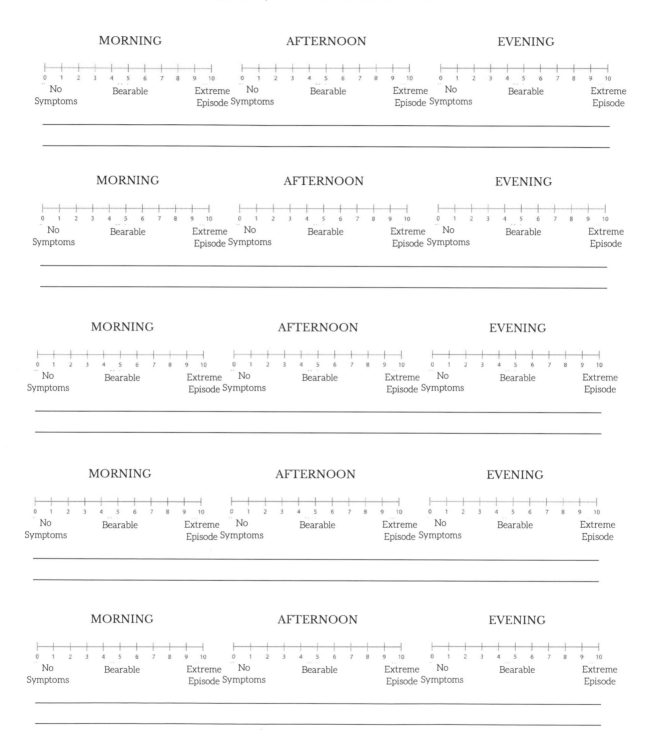

PAIN TRACKER BAR CHART

1

2

3

4

5

6

7

8

9

10

MONDAY	TUESDAY	WEDNESDAY	THURSDAY	FRIDAY	SATURDAY	SUNDAY

FOOD LOG AND FOOD TRIGGER TRACKER

FOOD	AMOUNT	TIME	IMMEDIATELY AFTER	1 HOUR	3 HOURS

LOG HOW YOU FEEL AFTER FOOD IN THESE SECTIONS

FOOD TRACKER

MEAL	MONDAY	TUESDAY	WEDNESDAY	THURSDAY	FRIDAY	SATURDAY	SUNDAY
BREAKFAST							
LUNCH							
DINNER							
CALORIES (OPTIONAL)							
SUPPLEMENTS	MULTIVIT ☐	MULTIVIT ☐	MULTIVIT ☐	MULTIVIT ☐	MULTIVIT ☐	MULTIVIT ☐	MULTIVIT ☐
	VITAMIN D ☐	VITAMIN D ☐	VITAMIN D ☐	VITAMIN D ☐	VITAMIN D ☐	VITAMIN D ☐	VITAMIN D ☐
	CALCIUM ☐	CALCIUM ☐	CALCIUM ☐	CALCIUM ☐	CALCIUM ☐	CALCIUM ☐	CALCIUM ☐
WATER INTAKE	☐☐☐☐ ☐☐☐	☐☐☐☐ ☐☐☐	☐☐☐☐ ☐☐☐	☐☐☐☐ ☐☐☐	☐☐☐☐ ☐☐☐	☐☐☐☐ ☐☐☐	☐☐☐☐ ☐☐☐

EXERCISE	MONDAY	TUESDAY	WEDNESDAY	THURSDAY	FRIDAY	SATURDAY	SUNDAY

FILL IN THE NOTES BELOW ON AREAS FOR IMPROVEMENT, SHOPPING LISTS, HOW YOU FELT AFTER YOU ATE, CALORIES, SNACKS AND WHATEVER YOU THINK WOULD BE USEFUL TO ADD TO YOUR FOOD JOURNAL

_____
_____
_____
_____
_____
_____
_____
_____
_____
_____

HOW OFTEN DID YOU FILL OUT THIS CHART
NOT AT ALL   [ ]   1-3X PER WEEK   [ ]   ALMOST EVERY DAY   [ ]   EVERYDAY   [ ]

MEDICATION & SUPPLEMENT TRACKER

MEDICATION NAME	DOSE.	MON	TUES	WED	THURS	FRI	SAT	SUN
EXAMPLE	5mg							

_____

_____

_____

_____

_____

_____

_____

_____

WHAT I HOPE IS YET TO COME...

ANSWER THESE QUESTIONS TO BREAK OUT OF NEGATIVE THOUGHT PATTERNS AND REFOCUS ON THE THINGS THAT MAKE YOU HAPPY AND GRATEFUL.

DAILY ENERGY vs MOOD TRACKER

TRACK YOUR DAILY ENERGY, MOOD AND ALSO PAIN USING DIFFERENT COLOURS ON THIS LINE CHART

100

75

50

25

0

| MONDAY | TUESDAY | WEDNESDAY | THURSDAY | FRIDAY | SATURDAY | SUNDAY |

NERGY

PAIN

TIME OF DAY PAIN TRACKER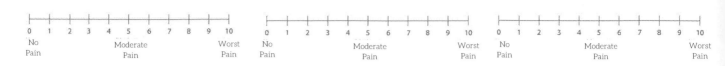

MORNING

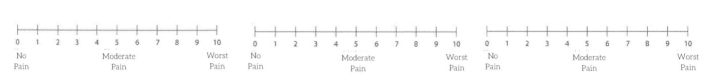

0 1 2 3 4 5 6 7 8 9 10

No Pain   Moderate Pain   Worst Pain

AFTERNOON

0 1 2 3 4 5 6 7 8 9 10

No Pain   Moderate Pain   Worst Pain

EVENING

0 1 2 3 4 5 6 7 8 9 10

No Pain   Moderate Pain   Worst Pain

MORNING

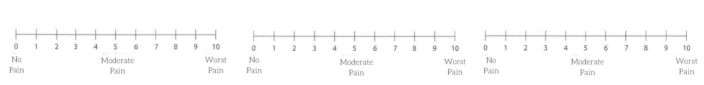

0 1 2 3 4 5 6 7 8 9 10

No Pain   Moderate Pain   Worst Pain

AFTERNOON

0 1 2 3 4 5 6 7 8 9 10

No Pain   Moderate Pain   Worst Pain

EVENING

0 1 2 3 4 5 6 7 8 9 10

No Pain   Moderate Pain   Worst Pain

MORNING

0 1 2 3 4 5 6 7 8 9 10

No Pain   Moderate Pain   Worst Pain

AFTERNOON

0 1 2 3 4 5 6 7 8 9 10

No Pain   Moderate Pain   Worst Pain

EVENING

0 1 2 3 4 5 6 7 8 9 10

No Pain   Moderate Pain   Worst Pain

MORNING

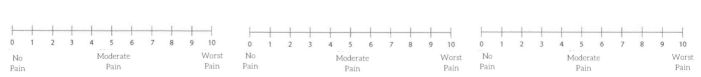

0 1 2 3 4 5 6 7 8 9 10

No Pain   Moderate Pain   Worst Pain

AFTERNOON

0 1 2 3 4 5 6 7 8 9 10

No Pain   Moderate Pain   Worst Pain

EVENING

0 1 2 3 4 5 6 7 8 9 10

No Pain   Moderate Pain   Worst Pain

MORNING

0 1 2 3 4 5 6 7 8 9 10

No Pain   Moderate Pain   Worst Pain

AFTERNOON

0 1 2 3 4 5 6 7 8 9 10

No Pain   Moderate Pain   Worst Pain

EVENING

0 1 2 3 4 5 6 7 8 9 10

No Pain   Moderate Pain   Worst Pain

SYMPTOM & TRIGGER TRACKER

	FREQ. / SEVERITY Y/N	MON	TUES	WED	THURS	FRI	SAT	SUN
DID YOU HAVE A GOOD DAY? (YES NO, 0-5 BAD TO GOOD)	Y/N 0-5	☐	☐	☐	☐	☐	☐	☐
MUSCLE PAIN OR WEAKNESS	0-5							
JOINT PAIN	0-5							
ENERGY LEVELS	0-5							
ANXIETY	0-5							
DIFFICULTY SLEEPING	0-5							
FEELING DEPRESSED / LOW MOOD	0-5							
OVER SLEEPING	Y/N							
DROWSIENESS	0-5							
HEADACHE / MIGRAINE	Y/N							
NAUSEA	0-5							
DIARRHOEA	0-5							
CONSTIPATION	Y-N							
BLOATING	0-5							
ACID REFLUX	Y/N							
NUMBNESS OR TINGLING	0-5							
HAIR LOSS	0-5							
SWOLLEN LYMPH NODES	0-5							
HEART PALPITATIONS	Y/N							
DRY EYES OR VISION PROBLEMS	0-5							
RINGING IN EARS	Y/N							
SENSITIVITY TO LIGHT	0-5							
SENSITIVITY TO SOUND	Y/N							
FACIAL NUMBNESS	Y/N							
BRAIN FOG / DIFFICULTY CONCENTRATING	Y/N							
HEADACHE OR MIGRAINE	Y/N							

CONTINUE TO THE NEXT PAGE

SYMPTOM & TRIGGER TRACKER

	FREQ. / SEVERITY Y/N	MON	TUES	WED	THURS	FRI	SAT	SUN
EXERCISE	MINS							
RASH	0-5							
MOUTH SORES	Y/N							
SKIN RASH	0-5							
UTI, DARK URINE OR OTHER BLADDER ISSUES	0-5							
LOW GRADE FEVER	TEMP							
COLD OR INFECTION	Y/N							
SHORTNESS OF BREATH	Y/N							
MEDICATION:	DOSE	☐	☐	☐	☐	☐	☐	☐
MEDICATION:	DOSE							
MEDICATION:	DOSE							
MEDICATION:	DOSE							

FILL IN THE CHARTS TO TRACK SYMPTOMS AND THEN PUT DETAILS AND POST POSSIBLE TRIGGERS IN THE NOTES BELOW.

_____
_____
_____
_____
_____
_____
_____
_____
_____
_____
_____
_____
_____

HOW OFTEN DID YOU FILL OUT THIS CHART

NOT AT ALL   [ ]   1-3X PER WEEK   [ ]   ALMOST EVERY DAY   [ ]   EVERYDAY   [ ]

SYMPTOM TRACKER

DATE	TIME	DURATION	DESCRIPTION
DATE	TIME	DURATION	DESCRIPTION

TIME OF DAY SYMPTOM TRACKER

TRACK THE SEVERITY OF YOUR SYMPTOMS THROUGHOUT THE DAY USING THE
SCALE, USE THE NOTE SECTION BELOW TO LIST THE SYMPTOMS YOU EXPERIENCED.
USE THIS TO SEE IF CERTAIN TIMES OF DAY E.G. MEAL TIMES OR FIRST THING IN THE
MORNING, ARE TRIGGERS FOR YOU.

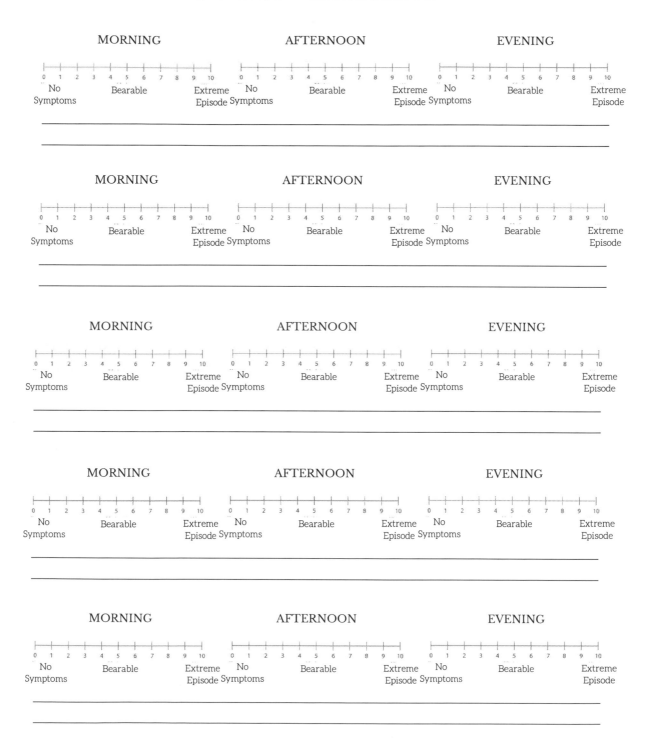

PAIN TRACKER BAR CHART

1

2

3

4

5

6

7

8

9

10

MONDAY	TUESDAY	WEDNESDAY	THURSDAY	FRIDAY	SATURDAY	SUNDAY

FOOD LOG AND FOOD TRIGGER TRACKER

FOOD	AMOUNT	TIME	IMMEDIATELY AFTER	1 HOUR	3 HOURS

LOG HOW YOU FEEL AFTER FOOD IN THESE SECTIONS

FOOD TRACKER

MEAL	MONDAY	TUESDAY	WEDNESDAY	THURSDAY	FRIDAY	SATURDAY	SUNDAY
BREAKFAST							
LUNCH							
DINNER							
CALORIES (OPTIONAL)							
SUPPLEMENTS	MULTIVIT ☐	MULTIVIT ☐	MULTIVIT ☐	MULTIVIT ☐	MULTIVIT ☐	MULTIVIT ☐	MULTIVIT ☐
	VITAMIN D ☐	VITAMIN D ☐	VITAMIN D ☐	VITAMIN D ☐	VITAMIN D ☐	VITAMIN D ☐	VITAMIN D ☐
	CALCIUM ☐	CALCIUM ☐	CALCIUM ☐	CALCIUM ☐	CALCIUM ☐	CALCIUM ☐	CALCIUM ☐
WATER INTAKE	☐☐☐ ☐☐☐	☐☐☐ ☐☐☐	☐☐☐ ☐☐☐	☐☐☐ ☐☐☐	☐☐☐ ☐☐☐	☐☐☐ ☐☐☐	☐☐☐ ☐☐☐

EXERCISE	MONDAY	TUESDAY	WEDNESDAY	THURSDAY	FRIDAY	SATURDAY	SUNDAY

FILL IN THE NOTES BELOW ON AREAS FOR IMPROVEMENT, SHOPPING LISTS, HOW YOU FELT AFTER YOU ATE, CALORIES, SNACKS AND WHATEVER YOU THINK WOULD BE USEFUL TO ADD TO YOUR FOOD JOURNAL

_____
_____
_____
_____
_____
_____
_____
_____
_____

HOW OFTEN DID YOU FILL OUT THIS CHART
NOT AT ALL   [ ]   1-3X PER WEEK   [ ]   ALMOST EVERY DAY   [ ]   EVERYDAY   [ ]

MEDICATION & SUPPLEMENT TRACKER

MEDICATION NAME	DOSE.	MON	TUES	WED	THURS	FRI	SAT	SUN
EXAMPLE	5mg							

_____

_____

_____

_____

_____

_____

_____

_____

It's okay to ask for help.

WHAT IS YOUR THE MOST DELICIOUS FOOD?

ANSWER THESE QUESTIONS TO BREAK OUT OF NEGATIVE
THOUGHT PATTERNS AND REFOCUS ON THE THINGS THAT MAKE
YOU HAPPY AND GRATEFUL.

DAILY ENERGY vs MOOD TRACKER

TRACK YOUR DAILY ENERGY, MOOD AND ALSO PAIN USING DIFFERENT COLOURS ON THIS LINE CHART

100

75

50

25

0

| MONDAY | TUESDAY | WEDNESDAY | THURSDAY | FRIDAY | SATURDAY | SUNDAY |

ENERGY

PAIN

TIME OF DAY PAIN TRACKER

MORNING

0 1 2 3 4 5 6 7 8 9 10
No Pain | Moderate Pain | Worst Pain

AFTERNOON

0 1 2 3 4 5 6 7 8 9 10
No Pain | Moderate Pain | Worst Pain

EVENING

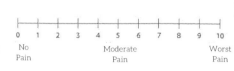
0 1 2 3 4 5 6 7 8 9 10
No Pain | Moderate Pain | Worst Pain

MORNING

0 1 2 3 4 5 6 7 8 9 10
No Pain | Moderate Pain | Worst Pain

AFTERNOON

0 1 2 3 4 5 6 7 8 9 10
No Pain | Moderate Pain | Worst Pain

EVENING

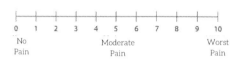
0 1 2 3 4 5 6 7 8 9 10
No Pain | Moderate Pain | Worst Pain

MORNING

0 1 2 3 4 5 6 7 8 9 10
No Pain | Moderate Pain | Worst Pain

AFTERNOON

0 1 2 3 4 5 6 7 8 9 10
No Pain | Moderate Pain | Worst Pain

EVENING

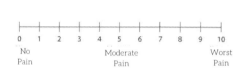
0 1 2 3 4 5 6 7 8 9 10
No Pain | Moderate Pain | Worst Pain

MORNING

0 1 2 3 4 5 6 7 8 9 10
No Pain | Moderate Pain | Worst Pain

AFTERNOON

0 1 2 3 4 5 6 7 8 9 10
No Pain | Moderate Pain | Worst Pain

EVENING

0 1 2 3 4 5 6 7 8 9 10
No Pain | Moderate Pain | Worst Pain

MORNING

0 1 2 3 4 5 6 7 8 9 10
No Pain | Moderate Pain | Worst Pain

AFTERNOON

0 1 2 3 4 5 6 7 8 9 10
No Pain | Moderate Pain | Worst Pain

EVENING

0 1 2 3 4 5 6 7 8 9 10
No Pain | Moderate Pain | Worst Pain

SYMPTOM & TRIGGER TRACKER

	FREQ. / SEVERITY Y/N	MON	TUES	WED	THURS	FRI	SAT	SUN
DID YOU HAVE A GOOD DAY? (YES NO, 0-5 BAD TO GOOD)	Y/N 0-5							
MUSCLE PAIN OR WEAKNESS	0-5							
JOINT PAIN	0-5							
ENERGY LEVELS	0-5							
ANXIETY	0-5							
DIFFICULTY SLEEPING	0-5							
FEELING DEPRESSED / LOW MOOD	0-5							
OVER SLEEPING	Y/N							
DROWSIENESS	0-5							
HEADACHE / MIGRAINE	Y/N							
NAUSEA	0-5							
DIARRHOEA	0-5							
CONSTIPATION	Y-N							
BLOATING	0-5							
ACID REFLUX	Y/N							
NUMBNESS OR TINGLING	0-5							
HAIR LOSS	0-5							
SWOLLEN LYMPH NODES	0-5							
HEART PALPITATIONS	Y/N							
DRY EYES OR VISION PROBLEMS	0-5							
RINGING IN EARS	Y/N							
SENSITIVITY TO LIGHT	0-5							
SENSITIVITY TO SOUND	Y/N							
FACIAL NUMBNESS	Y/N							
BRAIN FOG / DIFFICULTY CONCENTRATING	Y/N							
HEADACHE OR MIGRAINE	Y/N							

CONTINUE TO THE NEXT PAGE

SYMPTOM & TRIGGER TRACKER

	FREQ. / SEVERITY Y/N	MON	TUES	WED	THURS	FRI	SAT	SUN
EXERCISE	MINS							
RASH	0-5							
MOUTH SORES	Y/N							
SKIN RASH	0-5							
UTI, DARK URINE OR OTHER BLADDER ISSUES	0-5							
LOW GRADE FEVER	TEMP							
COLD OR INFECTION	Y/N							
SHORTNESS OF BREATH	Y/N							
MEDICATION:	DOSE	☐	☐	☐	☐	☐	☐	☐
MEDICATION:	DOSE							
MEDICATION:	DOSE							
MEDICATION:	DOSE							

FILL IN THE CHARTS TO TRACK SYMPTOMS AND THEN PUT DETAILS AND POST POSSIBLE TRIGGERS IN THE NOTES BELOW.

_____
_____
_____
_____
_____
_____
_____
_____
_____
_____
_____
_____
_____
_____

HOW OFTEN DID YOU FILL OUT THIS CHART

NOT AT ALL   [ ]   1-3X PER WEEK   [ ]   ALMOST EVERY DAY   [ ]   EVERYDAY   [ ]

SYMPTOM TRACKER

DATE	TIME	DURATION	DESCRIPTION
DATE	TIME	DURATION	DESCRIPTION

TIME OF DAY SYMPTOM TRACKER

TRACK THE SEVERITY OF YOUR SYMPTOMS THROUGHOUT THE DAY USING THE SCALE, USE THE NOTE SECTION BELOW TO LIST THE SYMPTOMS YOU EXPERIENCED. USE THIS TO SEE IF CERTAIN TIMES OF DAY E.G. MEAL TIMES OR FIRST THING IN THE MORNING, ARE TRIGGERS FOR YOU.

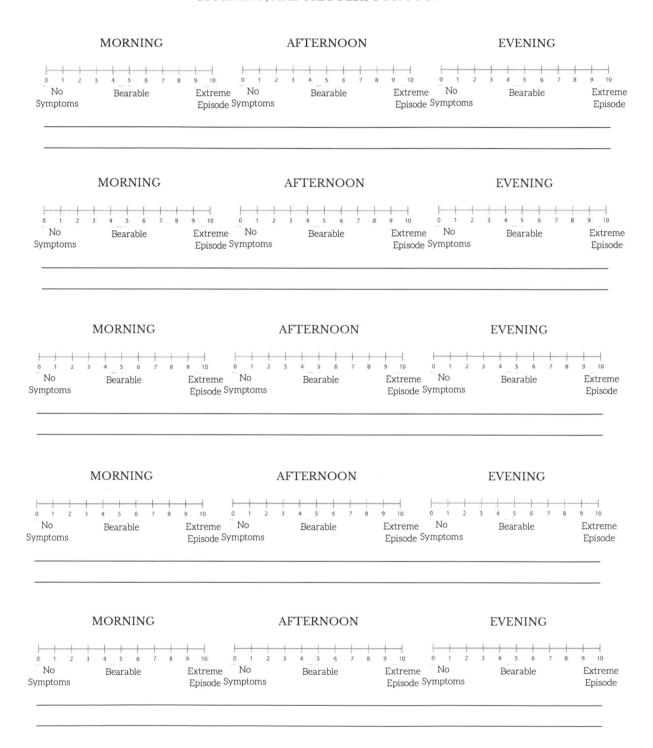

PAIN TRACKER BAR CHART

1

2

3

4

5

6

7

8

9

10

MONDAY	TUESDAY	WEDNESDAY	THURSDAY	FRIDAY	SATURDAY	SUNDAY

FOOD LOG AND FOOD TRIGGER TRACKER

FOOD	AMOUNT	TIME	IMMEDIATELY AFTER	1 HOUR	3 HOURS

LOG HOW YOU FEEL AFTER FOOD IN THESE SECTIONS

FOOD TRACKER

MEAL	MONDAY	TUESDAY	WEDNESDAY	THURSDAY	FRIDAY	SATURDAY	SUNDAY
BREAKFAST							
LUNCH							
DINNER							
CALORIES (OPTIONAL)							
SUPPLEMENTS	MULTIVIT [ ]	MULTIVIT [ ]	MULTIVIT [ ]	MULTIVIT [ ]	MULTIVIT [ ]	MULTIVIT [ ]	MULTIVIT [ ]
	VITAMIN D [ ]	VITAMIN D [ ]	VITAMIN D [ ]	VITAMIN D [ ]	VITAMIN D [ ]	VITAMIN D [ ]	VITAMIN D [ ]
	CALCIUM [ ]	CALCIUM [ ]	CALCIUM [ ]	CALCIUM [ ]	CALCIUM [ ]	CALCIUM [ ]	CALCIUM [ ]
WATER INTAKE							

EXERCISE	MONDAY	TUESDAY	WEDNESDAY	THURSDAY	FRIDAY	SATURDAY	SUNDAY

FILL IN THE NOTES BELOW ON AREAS FOR IMPROVEMENT, SHOPPING LISTS, HOW YOU FELT AFTER YOU ATE, CALORIES, SNACKS AND WHATEVER YOU THINK WOULD BE USEFUL TO ADD TO YOUR FOOD JOURNAL

_____

_____

_____

_____

_____

_____

_____

_____

_____

HOW OFTEN DID YOU FILL OUT THIS CHART
NOT AT ALL   [ ]   1-3X PER WEEK   [ ]   ALMOST EVERY DAY   [ ]   EVERYDAY   [ ]

MEDICATION & SUPPLEMENT TRACKER

MEDICATION NAME	DOSE.	MON	TUES	WED	THURS	FRI	SAT	SUN
EXAMPLE	5mg							

_____

_____

_____

_____

_____

_____

_____

_____

YOU ARE
STRONGER
THAN
THE STRUGGLE

WHAT DO YOU LOVE ABOUT YOUR FAVOURITE BOOK

ANSWER THESE QUESTIONS TO BREAK OUT OF NEGATIVE THOUGHT PATTERNS AND REFOCUS ON THE THINGS THAT MAKE YOU HAPPY AND GRATEFUL.

DAILY ENERGY vs MOOD TRACKER

TRACK YOUR DAILY ENERGY, MOOD AND ALSO PAIN USING DIFFERENT COLOURS ON THIS LINE CHART

	MONDAY	TUESDAY	WEDNESDAY	THURSDAY	FRIDAY	SATURDAY	SUNDAY	
100								
75								
50								
25								
0								

ENERGY

PAIN

TIME OF DAY PAIN TRACKER

MORNING

0 1 2 3 4 5 6 7 8 9 10
No Pain   Moderate Pain   Worst Pain

AFTERNOON

0 1 2 3 4 5 6 7 8 9 10
No Pain   Moderate Pain   Worst Pain

EVENING

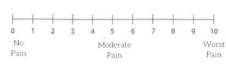

0 1 2 3 4 5 6 7 8 9 10
No Pain   Moderate Pain   Worst Pain

MORNING

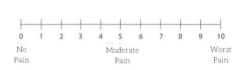

0 1 2 3 4 5 6 7 8 9 10
No Pain   Moderate Pain   Worst Pain

AFTERNOON

0 1 2 3 4 5 6 7 8 9 10
No Pain   Moderate Pain   Worst Pain

EVENING

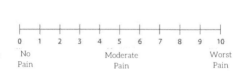

0 1 2 3 4 5 6 7 8 9 10
No Pain   Moderate Pain   Worst Pain

MORNING

0 1 2 3 4 5 6 7 8 9 10
No Pain   Moderate Pain   Worst Pain

AFTERNOON

0 1 2 3 4 5 6 7 8 9 10
No Pain   Moderate Pain   Worst Pain

EVENING

0 1 2 3 4 5 6 7 8 9 10
No Pain   Moderate Pain   Worst Pain

MORNING

0 1 2 3 4 5 6 7 8 9 10
No Pain   Moderate Pain   Worst Pain

AFTERNOON

0 1 2 3 4 5 6 7 8 9 10
No Pain   Moderate Pain   Worst Pain

EVENING

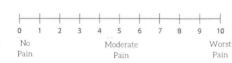

0 1 2 3 4 5 6 7 8 9 10
No Pain   Moderate Pain   Worst Pain

MORNING

0 1 2 3 4 5 6 7 8 9 10
No Pain   Moderate Pain   Worst Pain

AFTERNOON

0 1 2 3 4 5 6 7 8 9 10
No Pain   Moderate Pain   Worst Pain

EVENING

0 1 2 3 4 5 6 7 8 9 10
No Pain   Moderate Pain   Worst Pain

SYMPTOM & TRIGGER TRACKER

	FREQ. / SEVERITY Y/N	MON	TUES	WED	THURS	FRI	SAT	SUN
DID YOU HAVE A GOOD DAY? (YES NO, 0-5 BAD TO GOOD)	Y/N 0-5							
MUSCLE PAIN OR WEAKNESS	0-5							
JOINT PAIN	0-5							
ENERGY LEVELS	0-5							
ANXIETY	0-5							
DIFFICULTY SLEEPING	0-5							
FEELING DEPRESSED / LOW MOOD	0-5							
OVER SLEEPING	Y/N							
DROWSIENESS	0-5							
HEADACHE / MIGRAINE	Y/N							
NAUSEA	0-5							
DIARRHOEA	0-5							
CONSTIPATION	Y-N							
BLOATING	0-5							
ACID REFLUX	Y/N							
NUMBNESS OR TINGLING	0-5							
HAIR LOSS	0-5							
SWOLLEN LYMPH NODES	0-5							
HEART PALPITATIONS	Y/N							
DRY EYES OR VISION PROBLEMS	0-5							
RINGING IN EARS	Y/N							
SENSITIVITY TO LIGHT	0-5							
SENSITIVITY TO SOUND	Y/N							
FACIAL NUMBNESS	Y/N							
BRAIN FOG / DIFFICULTY CONCENTRATING	Y/N							
HEADACHE OR MIGRAINE	Y/N							

CONTINUE TO THE NEXT PAGE

SYMPTOM & TRIGGER TRACKER

	FREQ. / SEVERITY Y/N	MON	TUES	WED	THURS	FRI	SAT	SUN
EXERCISE	MINS							
RASH	0-5							
MOUTH SORES	Y/N							
SKIN RASH	0-5							
UTI, DARK URINE OR OTHER BLADDER ISSUES	0-5							
LOW GRADE FEVER	TEMP							
COLD OR INFECTION	Y/N							
SHORTNESS OF BREATH	Y/N							
MEDICATION:	DOSE							
MEDICATION:	DOSE							
MEDICATION:	DOSE							
MEDICATION:	DOSE							

FILL IN THE CHARTS TO TRACK SYMPTOMS AND THEN PUT DETAILS AND POST POSSIBLE TRIGGERS IN THE NOTES BELOW.

_____
_____
_____
_____
_____
_____
_____
_____
_____
_____
_____
_____

HOW OFTEN DID YOU FILL OUT THIS CHART

NOT AT ALL   [ ]   1-3X PER WEEK   [ ]   ALMOST EVERY DAY   [ ]   EVERYDAY   [ ]

SYMPTOM TRACKER

DATE	TIME	DURATION	DESCRIPTION

TIME OF DAY SYMPTOM TRACKER

TRACK THE SEVERITY OF YOUR SYMPTOMS THROUGHOUT THE DAY USING THE
SCALE, USE THE NOTE SECTION BELOW TO LIST THE SYMPTOMS YOU EXPERIENCED.
USE THIS TO SEE IF CERTAIN TIMES OF DAY E.G. MEAL TIMES OR FIRST THING IN THE
MORNING, ARE TRIGGERS FOR YOU.

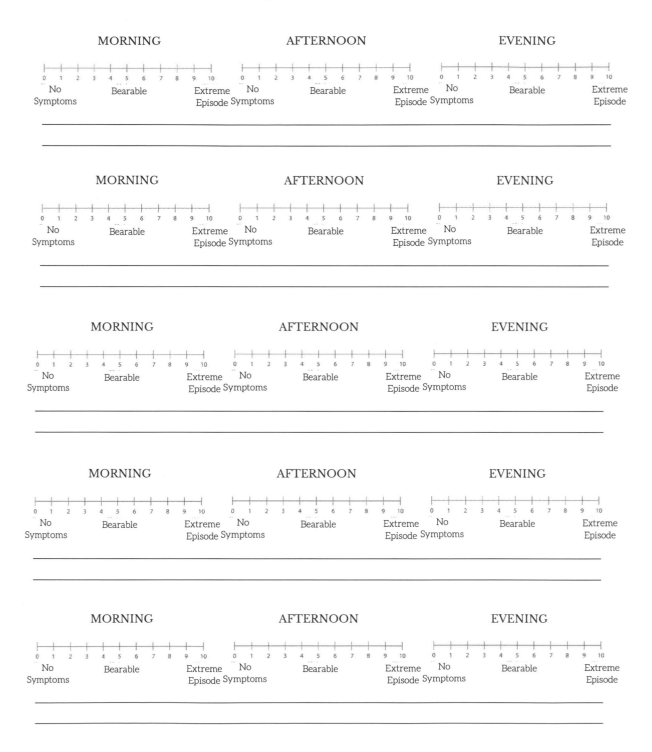

PAIN TRACKER BAR CHART

1
2
3
4
5
6
7
8
9
10

MONDAY	TUESDAY	WEDNESDAY	THURSDAY	FRIDAY	SATURDAY	SUNDAY

FOOD LOG AND FOOD TRIGGER TRACKER

FOOD	AMOUNT	TIME	IMMEDIATELY AFTER	1 HOUR	3 HOURS

LOG HOW YOU FEEL AFTER FOOD IN THESE SECTIONS

FOOD TRACKER

MEAL	MONDAY	TUESDAY	WEDNESDAY	THURSDAY	FRIDAY	SATURDAY	SUNDAY
BREAKFAST							
LUNCH							
DINNER							
CALORIES (OPTIONAL)							
SUPPLEMENTS	MULTIVIT [ ]	MULTIVIT [ ]	MULTIVIT [ ]	MULTIVIT [ ]	MULTIVIT [ ]	MULTIVIT [ ]	MULTIVIT [ ]
	VITAMIN D [ ]	VITAMIN D [ ]	VITAMIN D [ ]	VITAMIN D [ ]	VITAMIN D [ ]	VITAMIN D [ ]	VITAMIN D [ ]
	CALCIUM [ ]	CALCIUM [ ]	CALCIUM [ ]	CALCIUM [ ]	CALCIUM [ ]	CALCIUM [ ]	CALCIUM [ ]
WATER INTAKE							

EXERCISE	MONDAY	TUESDAY	WEDNESDAY	THURSDAY	FRIDAY	SATURDAY	SUNDAY

FILL IN THE NOTES BELOW ON AREAS FOR IMPROVEMENT, SHOPPING LISTS, HOW YOU FELT AFTER YOU ATE, CALORIES, SNACKS AND WHATEVER YOU THINK WOULD BE USEFUL TO ADD TO YOUR FOOD JOURNAL

_____

_____

_____

_____

_____

_____

_____

_____

_____

_____

HOW OFTEN DID YOU FILL OUT THIS CHART
NOT AT ALL   [ ]   1-3X PER WEEK   [ ]   ALMOST EVERY DAY   [ ]   EVERYDAY   [ ]

MEDICATION & SUPPLEMENT TRACKER

MEDICATION NAME	DOSE.	MON	TUES	WED	THURS	FRI	SAT	SUN
EXAMPLE	5mg							

_____

_____

_____

_____

_____

_____

_____

_____

"Recovery is about progress not perfection."

WHY IS IT IMPORTANT TO HAVE GOOD SELF-ESTEEM?

ANSWER THESE QUESTIONS TO BREAK OUT OF NEGATIVE THOUGHT PATTERNS AND REFOCUS ON THE THINGS THAT MAKE YOU LOVE LIFE AND LOVE YOURSELF!

_____
_____
_____
_____
_____
_____
_____
_____
_____
_____
_____
_____
_____
_____
_____
_____
_____
_____
_____
_____

DAILY ENERGY vs MOOD TRACKER

TRACK YOUR DAILY ENERGY, MOOD AND ALSO PAIN USING DIFFERENT COLOURS ON THIS LINE CHART

100

75

50

25

0

ENERGY

MONDAY   TUESDAY   WEDNESDAY   THURSDAY   FRIDAY   SATURDAY   SUNDAY

PAIN

TIME OF DAY PAIN TRACKER

MORNING

0 1 2 3 4 5 6 7 8 9 10
No Pain   Moderate Pain   Worst Pain

AFTERNOON

0 1 2 3 4 5 6 7 8 9 10
No Pain   Moderate Pain   Worst Pain

EVENING

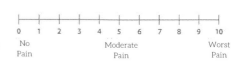

0 1 2 3 4 5 6 7 8 9 10
No Pain   Moderate Pain   Worst Pain

MORNING

0 1 2 3 4 5 6 7 8 9 10
No Pain   Moderate Pain   Worst Pain

AFTERNOON

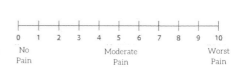

0 1 2 3 4 5 6 7 8 9 10
No Pain   Moderate Pain   Worst Pain

EVENING

0 1 2 3 4 5 6 7 8 9 10
No Pain   Moderate Pain   Worst Pain

MORNING

0 1 2 3 4 5 6 7 8 9 10
No Pain   Moderate Pain   Worst Pain

AFTERNOON

0 1 2 3 4 5 6 7 8 9 10
No Pain   Moderate Pain   Worst Pain

EVENING

0 1 2 3 4 5 6 7 8 9 10
No Pain   Moderate Pain   Worst Pain

MORNING

0 1 2 3 4 5 6 7 8 9 10
No Pain   Moderate Pain   Worst Pain

AFTERNOON

0 1 2 3 4 5 6 7 8 9 10
No Pain   Moderate Pain   Worst Pain

EVENING

0 1 2 3 4 5 6 7 8 9 10
No Pain   Moderate Pain   Worst Pain

MORNING

0 1 2 3 4 5 6 7 8 9 10
No Pain   Moderate Pain   Worst Pain

AFTERNOON

0 1 2 3 4 5 6 7 8 9 10
No Pain   Moderate Pain   Worst Pain

EVENING

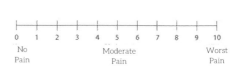

0 1 2 3 4 5 6 7 8 9 10
No Pain   Moderate Pain   Worst Pain

SYMPTOM & TRIGGER TRACKER

	FREQ. / SEVERITY Y/N	MON	TUES	WED	THURS	FRI	SAT	SUN
DID YOU HAVE A GOOD DAY? (YES NO, 0-5 BAD TO GOOD)	Y/N 0-5							
MUSCLE PAIN OR WEAKNESS	0-5							
JOINT PAIN	0-5							
ENERGY LEVELS	0-5							
ANXIETY	0-5							
DIFFICULTY SLEEPING	0-5							
FEELING DEPRESSED / LOW MOOD	0-5							
OVER SLEEPING	Y/N							
DROWSIENESS	0-5							
HEADACHE / MIGRAINE	Y/N							
NAUSEA	0-5							
DIARRHOEA	0-5							
CONSTIPATION	Y-N							
BLOATING	0-5							
ACID REFLUX	Y/N							
NUMBNESS OR TINGLING	0-5							
HAIR LOSS	0-5							
SWOLLEN LYMPH NODES	0-5							
HEART PALPITATIONS	Y/N							
DRY EYES OR VISION PROBLEMS	0-5							
RINGING IN EARS	Y/N							
SENSITIVITY TO LIGHT	0-5							
SENSITIVITY TO SOUND	Y/N							
FACIAL NUMBNESS	Y/N							
BRAIN FOG / DIFFICULTY CONCENTRATING	Y/N							
HEADACHE OR MIGRAINE	Y/N							

CONTINUE TO THE NEXT PAGE

SYMPTOM & TRIGGER TRACKER

	FREQ. / SEVERITY Y/N	MON	TUES	WED	THURS	FRI	SAT	SUN
EXERCISE	MINS							
RASH	0-5							
MOUTH SORES	Y/N							
SKIN RASH	0-5							
UTI, DARK URINE OR OTHER BLADDER ISSUES	0-5							
LOW GRADE FEVER	TEMP							
COLD OR INFECTION	Y/N							
SHORTNESS OF BREATH	Y/N							
MEDICATION:	DOSE	☐	☐	☐	☐	☐	☐	☐
MEDICATION:	DOSE							
MEDICATION:	DOSE							
MEDICATION:	DOSE							

FILL IN THE CHARTS TO TRACK SYMPTOMS AND THEN PUT DETAILS AND POST POSSIBLE TRIGGERS IN THE NOTES BELOW.

_____
_____
_____
_____
_____
_____
_____
_____
_____
_____
_____
_____
_____
_____

HOW OFTEN DID YOU FILL OUT THIS CHART
NOT AT ALL   [ ]   1-3X PER WEEK   [ ]   ALMOST EVERY DAY   [ ]   EVERYDAY   [ ]

SYMPTOM TRACKER

DATE	TIME	DURATION	DESCRIPTION
DATE	TIME	DURATION	DESCRIPTION

TIME OF DAY SYMPTOM TRACKER

TRACK THE SEVERITY OF YOUR SYMPTOMS THROUGHOUT THE DAY USING THE
SCALE, USE THE NOTE SECTION BELOW TO LIST THE SYMPTOMS YOU EXPERIENCED.
USE THIS TO SEE IF CERTAIN TIMES OF DAY E.G. MEAL TIMES OR FIRST THING IN THE
MORNING, ARE TRIGGERS FOR YOU.

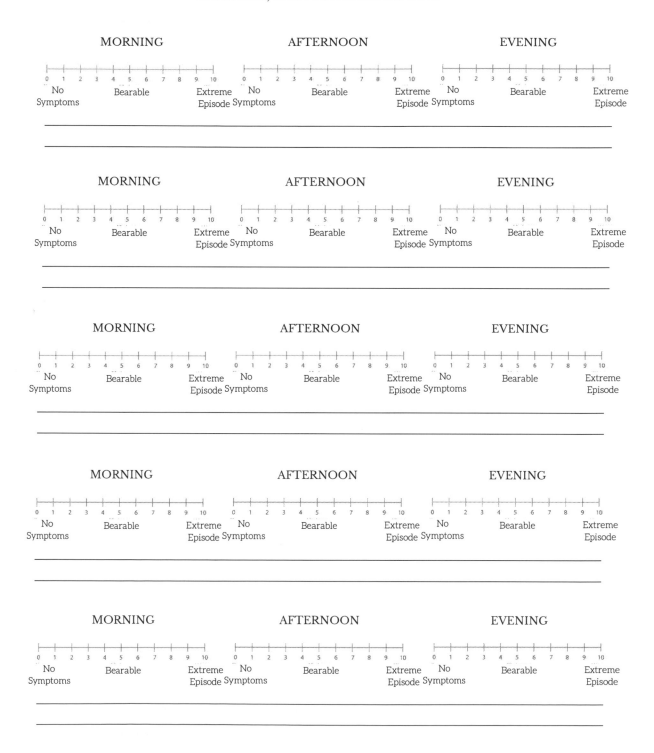

PAIN TRACKER BAR CHART

1

2

3

4

5

6

7

8

9

10

MONDAY	TUESDAY	WEDNESDAY	THURSDAY	FRIDAY	SATURDAY	SUNDAY

FOOD LOG AND FOOD TRIGGER TRACKER

FOOD	AMOUNT	TIME	IMMEDIATELY AFTER	1 HOUR	3 HOURS

LOG HOW YOU FEEL AFTER FOOD IN THESE SECTIONS

FOOD TRACKER

MEAL	MONDAY	TUESDAY	WEDNESDAY	THURSDAY	FRIDAY	SATURDAY	SUNDAY
BREAKFAST							
LUNCH							
DINNER							
CALORIES (OPTIONAL)							
SUPPLEMENTS	MULTIVIT ☐	MULTIVIT ☐	MULTIVIT ☐	MULTIVIT ☐	MULTIVIT ☐	MULTIVIT ☐	MULTIVIT ☐
	VITAMIN D ☐	VITAMIN D ☐	VITAMIN D ☐	VITAMIN D ☐	VITAMIN D ☐	VITAMIN D ☐	VITAMIN D ☐
	CALCIUM ☐	CALCIUM ☐	CALCIUM ☐	CALCIUM ☐	CALCIUM ☐	CALCIUM ☐	CALCIUM ☐
WATER INTAKE	☐☐☐ ☐☐☐	☐☐☐ ☐☐☐	☐☐☐ ☐☐☐	☐☐☐ ☐☐☐	☐☐☐ ☐☐☐	☐☐☐ ☐☐☐	☐☐☐ ☐☐☐

EXERCISE	MONDAY	TUESDAY	WEDNESDAY	THURSDAY	FRIDAY	SATURDAY	SUNDAY

FILL IN THE NOTES BELOW ON AREAS FOR IMPROVEMENT, SHOPPING LISTS, HOW YOU FELT AFTER YOU ATE, CALORIES, SNACKS AND WHATEVER YOU THINK WOULD BE USEFUL TO ADD TO YOUR FOOD JOURNAL

_____

_____

_____

_____

_____

_____

_____

_____

_____

_____

HOW OFTEN DID YOU FILL OUT THIS CHART
NOT AT ALL   [ ]   1-3X PER WEEK   [ ]   ALMOST EVERY DAY   [ ]   EVERYDAY   [ ]

MEDICATION & SUPPLEMENT TRACKER

MEDICATION NAME	DOSE.	MON	TUES	WED	THURS	FRI	SAT	SUN
EXAMPLE	5mg							

_____

_____

_____

_____

_____

_____

_____

_____

Make Your Head A Nice Place To Live.

DAILY ENERGY vs MOOD TRACKER

TRACK YOUR DAILY ENERGY, MOOD AND ALSO PAIN USING DIFFERENT COLOURS ON THIS LINE CHART

ENERGY		MONDAY	TUESDAY	WEDNESDAY	THURSDAY	FRIDAY	SATURDAY	SUNDAY	PAIN
100									
75									
50									
25									
0									

TIME OF DAY PAIN TRACKER

MORNING

0 1 2 3 4 5 6 7 8 9 10

No
Pain

Moderate
Pain

Worst
Pain

AFTERNOON

0 1 2 3 4 5 6 7 8 9 10

No
Pain

Moderate
Pain

Worst
Pain

EVENING

0 1 2 3 4 5 6 7 8 9 10

No
Pain

Moderate
Pain

Worst
Pain

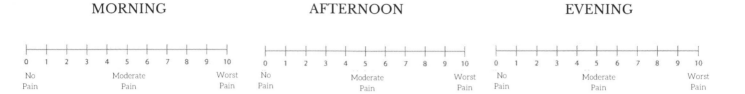

MORNING

0 1 2 3 4 5 6 7 8 9 10

No
Pain

Moderate
Pain

Worst
Pain

AFTERNOON

0 1 2 3 4 5 6 7 8 9 10

No
Pain

Moderate
Pain

Worst
Pain

EVENING

0 1 2 3 4 5 6 7 8 9 10

No
Pain

Moderate
Pain

Worst
Pain

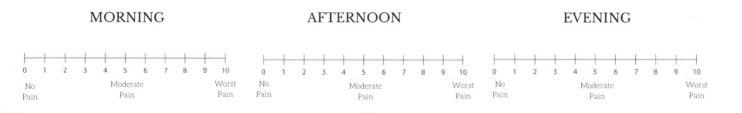

MORNING

0 1 2 3 4 5 6 7 8 9 10

No
Pain

Moderate
Pain

Worst
Pain

AFTERNOON

0 1 2 3 4 5 6 7 8 9 10

No
Pain

Moderate
Pain

Worst
Pain

EVENING

0 1 2 3 4 5 6 7 8 9 10

No
Pain

Moderate
Pain

Worst
Pain

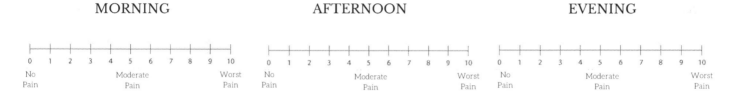

MORNING

0 1 2 3 4 5 6 7 8 9 10

No
Pain

Moderate
Pain

Worst
Pain

AFTERNOON

0 1 2 3 4 5 6 7 8 9 10

No
Pain

Moderate
Pain

Worst
Pain

EVENING

0 1 2 3 4 5 6 7 8 9 10

No
Pain

Moderate
Pain

Worst
Pain

MORNING

0 1 2 3 4 5 6 7 8 9 10

No
Pain

Moderate
Pain

Worst
Pain

AFTERNOON

0 1 2 3 4 5 6 7 8 9 10

No
Pain

Moderate
Pain

Worst
Pain

EVENING

0 1 2 3 4 5 6 7 8 9 10

No
Pain

Moderate
Pain

Worst
Pain

SYMPTOM & TRIGGER TRACKER

	FREQ. / SEVERITY Y/N	MON	TUES	WED	THURS	FRI	SAT	SUN
DID YOU HAVE A GOOD DAY? (YES NO, 0-5 BAD TO GOOD)	Y/N 0-5	☐	☐	☐	☐	☐	☐	☐
MUSCLE PAIN OR WEAKNESS	0-5							
JOINT PAIN	0-5							
ENERGY LEVELS	0-5							
ANXIETY	0-5							
DIFFICULTY SLEEPING	0-5							
FEELING DEPRESSED / LOW MOOD	0-5							
OVER SLEEPING	Y/N							
DROWSIENESS	0-5							
HEADACHE / MIGRAINE	Y/N							
NAUSEA	0-5							
DIARRHOEA	0-5							
CONSTIPATION	Y-N							
BLOATING	0-5							
ACID REFLUX	Y/N							
NUMBNESS OR TINGLING	0-5							
HAIR LOSS	0-5							
SWOLLEN LYMPH NODES	0-5							
HEART PALPITATIONS	Y/N							
DRY EYES OR VISION PROBLEMS	0-5							
RINGING IN EARS	Y/N							
SENSITIVITY TO LIGHT	0-5							
SENSITIVITY TO SOUND	Y/N							
FACIAL NUMBNESS	Y/N							
BRAIN FOG / DIFFICULTY CONCENTRATING	Y/N							
HEADACHE OR MIGRAINE	Y/N							

CONTINUE TO THE NEXT PAGE

SYMPTOM & TRIGGER TRACKER

	FREQ. / SEVERITY Y/N	MON	TUES	WED	THURS	FRI	SAT	SUN
EXERCISE	MINS							
RASH	0-5							
MOUTH SORES	Y/N							
SKIN RASH	0-5							
UTI, DARK URINE OR OTHER BLADDER ISSUES	0-5							
LOW GRADE FEVER	TEMP							
COLD OR INFECTION	Y/N							
SHORTNESS OF BREATH	Y/N							
MEDICATION:	DOSE	☐	☐	☐	☐	☐	☐	☐
MEDICATION:	DOSE							
MEDICATION:	DOSE							
MEDICATION:	DOSE							

FILL IN THE CHARTS TO TRACK SYMPTOMS AND THEN PUT DETAILS AND POST POSSIBLE TRIGGERS IN THE NOTES BELOW.

_____
_____
_____
_____
_____
_____
_____
_____
_____
_____
_____
_____
_____

HOW OFTEN DID YOU FILL OUT THIS CHART

NOT AT ALL   [ ]   1-3X PER WEEK   [ ]   ALMOST EVERY DAY   [ ]   EVERYDAY   [ ]

SYMPTOM TRACKER

DATE	TIME	DURATION	DESCRIPTION

TIME OF DAY SYMPTOM TRACKER

TRACK THE SEVERITY OF YOUR SYMPTOMS THROUGHOUT THE DAY USING THE SCALE, USE THE NOTE SECTION BELOW TO LIST THE SYMPTOMS YOU EXPERIENCED. USE THIS TO SEE IF CERTAIN TIMES OF DAY E.G. MEAL TIMES OR FIRST THING IN THE MORNING, ARE TRIGGERS FOR YOU.

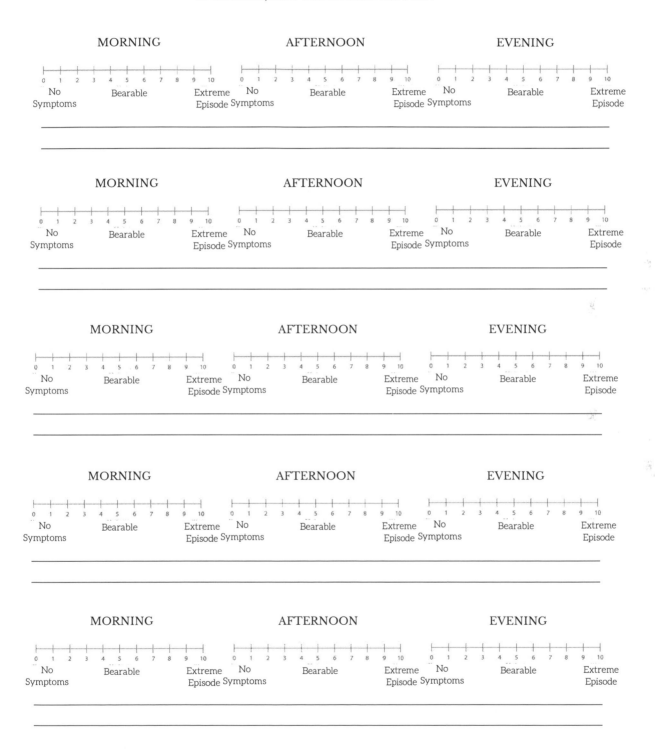

PAIN TRACKER BAR CHART

1

2

3

4

5

6

7

8

9

10

MONDAY	TUESDAY	WEDNESDAY	THURSDAY	FRIDAY	SATURDAY	SUNDAY

⟳ TURN BOOK TO USE THIS PAGE

FOOD LOG AND FOOD TRIGGER TRACKER

FOOD	AMOUNT	TIME	IMMEDIATELY AFTER	1 HOUR	3 HOURS

LOG HOW YOU FEEL AFTER FOOD IN THESE SECTIONS

FOOD TRACKER

MEAL	MONDAY	TUESDAY	WEDNESDAY	THURSDAY	FRIDAY	SATURDAY	SUNDAY
BREAKFAST							
LUNCH							
DINNER							
CALORIES (OPTIONAL)							
SUPPLEMENTS	MULTIVIT [ ] VITAMIN D [ ] CALCIUM [ ]	MULTIVIT [ ] VITAMIN D [ ] CALCIUM [ ]	MULTIVIT [ ] VITAMIN D [ ] CALCIUM [ ]	MULTIVIT [ ] VITAMIN D [ ] CALCIUM [ ]	MULTIVIT [ ] VITAMIN D [ ] CALCIUM [ ]	MULTIVIT [ ] VITAMIN D [ ] CALCIUM [ ]	MULTIVIT [ ] VITAMIN D [ ] CALCIUM [ ]
WATER INTAKE							

EXERCISE	MONDAY	TUESDAY	WEDNESDAY	THURSDAY	FRIDAY	SATURDAY	SUNDAY

FILL IN THE NOTES BELOW ON AREAS FOR IMPROVEMENT, SHOPPING LISTS, HOW YOU FELT AFTER YOU ATE, CALORIES, SNACKS AND WHATEVER YOU THINK WOULD BE USEFUL TO ADD TO YOUR FOOD JOURNAL

_____

_____

_____

_____

_____

_____

_____

_____

_____

HOW OFTEN DID YOU FILL OUT THIS CHART

NOT AT ALL   [ ]   1-3X PER WEEK   [ ]   ALMOST EVERY DAY   [ ]   EVERYDAY   [ ]

MEDICATION & SUPPLEMENT TRACKER

MEDICATION NAME	DOSE.	MON	TUES	WED	THURS	FRI	SAT	SUN
EXAMPLE	5mg							

_____

_____

_____

_____

_____

_____

_____

AFFIRMATION #2
Try adding
"and that's okay"
to any negative thought you have.

I need other people's help
...and that's okay.

I have so much more left to do
...and that's okay

Tomorrow is a new day.
Don't waste energy feeling bad.
Use it to move forward.

DESCRIBE THREE THINGS YOU LOVE ABOUT YOURSELF.

ANSWER THESE QUESTIONS TO BREAK OUT OF NEGATIVE THOUGHT PATTERNS AND REFOCUS ON THE THINGS THAT MAKE YOU LOVE LIFE AND LOVE YOURSELF!

_____

_____

_____

_____

_____

_____

_____

_____

_____

DAILY ENERGY vs MOOD TRACKER

TRACK YOUR DAILY ENERGY, MOOD AND ALSO PAIN USING DIFFERENT COLOURS ON THIS LINE CHART

	100

| | 75 |

| | 50 |

| | 25 |

| | 0 | MONDAY | TUESDAY | WEDNESDAY | THURSDAY | FRIDAY | SATURDAY | SUNDAY |

ENERGY

PAIN

TIME OF DAY PAIN TRACKER

MORNING	AFTERNOON	EVENING
0 1 2 3 4 5 6 7 8 9 10	0 1 2 3 4 5 6 7 8 9 10	0 1 2 3 4 5 6 7 8 9 10
No Pain / Moderate Pain / Worst Pain	No Pain / Moderate Pain / Worst Pain	No Pain / Moderate Pain / Worst Pain

MORNING	AFTERNOON	EVENING
0 1 2 3 4 5 6 7 8 9 10	0 1 2 3 4 5 6 7 8 9 10	0 1 2 3 4 5 6 7 8 9 10
No Pain / Moderate Pain / Worst Pain	No Pain / Moderate Pain / Worst Pain	No Pain / Moderate Pain / Worst Pain

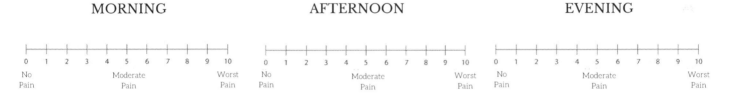

MORNING	AFTERNOON	EVENING
0 1 2 3 4 5 6 7 8 9 10	0 1 2 3 4 5 6 7 8 9 10	0 1 2 3 4 5 6 7 8 9 10
No Pain / Moderate Pain / Worst Pain	No Pain / Moderate Pain / Worst Pain	No Pain / Moderate Pain / Worst Pain

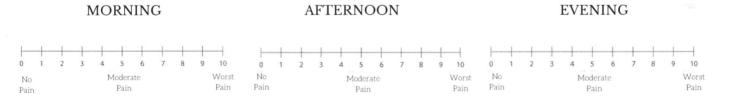

MORNING	AFTERNOON	EVENING
0 1 2 3 4 5 6 7 8 9 10	0 1 2 3 4 5 6 7 8 9 10	0 1 2 3 4 5 6 7 8 9 10
No Pain / Moderate Pain / Worst Pain	No Pain / Moderate Pain / Worst Pain	No Pain / Moderate Pain / Worst Pain

MORNING	AFTERNOON	EVENING
0 1 2 3 4 5 6 7 8 9 10	0 1 2 3 4 5 6 7 8 9 10	0 1 2 3 4 5 6 7 8 9 10
No Pain / Moderate Pain / Worst Pain	No Pain / Moderate Pain / Worst Pain	No Pain / Moderate Pain / Worst Pain

SYMPTOM & TRIGGER TRACKER

	FREQ. / SEVERITY Y/N	MON	TUES	WED	THURS	FRI	SAT	SUN
DID YOU HAVE A GOOD DAY? (YES NO, 0-5 BAD TO GOOD)	Y/N 0-5	☐	☐	☐	☐	☐	☐	☐
MUSCLE PAIN OR WEAKNESS	0-5							
JOINT PAIN	0-5							
ENERGY LEVELS	0-5							
ANXIETY	0-5							
DIFFICULTY SLEEPING	0-5							
FEELING DEPRESSED / LOW MOOD	0-5							
OVER SLEEPING	Y/N							
DROWSIENESS	0-5							
HEADACHE / MIGRAINE	Y/N							
NAUSEA	0-5							
DIARRHOEA	0-5							
CONSTIPATION	Y-N							
BLOATING	0-5							
ACID REFLUX	Y/N							
NUMBNESS OR TINGLING	0-5							
HAIR LOSS	0-5							
SWOLLEN LYMPH NODES	0-5							
HEART PALPITATIONS	Y/N							
DRY EYES OR VISION PROBLEMS	0-5							
RINGING IN EARS	Y/N							
SENSITIVITY TO LIGHT	0-5							
SENSITIVITY TO SOUND	Y/N							
FACIAL NUMBNESS	Y/N							
BRAIN FOG / DIFFICULTY CONCENTRATING	Y/N							
HEADACHE OR MIGRAINE	Y/N							

CONTINUE TO THE NEXT PAGE

SYMPTOM & TRIGGER TRACKER

	FREQ. / SEVERITY Y/N	MON	TUES	WED	THURS	FRI	SAT	SUN
EXERCISE	MINS							
RASH	0-5							
MOUTH SORES	Y/N							
SKIN RASH	0-5							
UTI, DARK URINE OR OTHER BLADDER ISSUES	0-5							
LOW GRADE FEVER	TEMP							
COLD OR INFECTION	Y/N							
SHORTNESS OF BREATH	Y/N							
MEDICATION:	DOSE	☐	☐	☐	☐	☐	☐	☐
MEDICATION:	DOSE							
MEDICATION:	DOSE							
MEDICATION:	DOSE							

FILL IN THE CHARTS TO TRACK SYMPTOMS AND THEN PUT DETAILS AND POST POSSIBLE TRIGGERS IN THE NOTES BELOW.

_____
_____
_____
_____
_____
_____
_____
_____
_____
_____
_____
_____
_____

HOW OFTEN DID YOU FILL OUT THIS CHART

NOT AT ALL [ ]   1-3X PER WEEK [ ]   ALMOST EVERY DAY [ ]   EVERYDAY [ ]

SYMPTOM TRACKER

DATE	TIME	DURATION	DESCRIPTION

TIME OF DAY SYMPTOM TRACKER

TRACK THE SEVERITY OF YOUR SYMPTOMS THROUGHOUT THE DAY USING THE
SCALE, USE THE NOTE SECTION BELOW TO LIST THE SYMPTOMS YOU EXPERIENCED.
USE THIS TO SEE IF CERTAIN TIMES OF DAY E.G. MEAL TIMES OR FIRST THING IN THE
MORNING, ARE TRIGGERS FOR YOU.

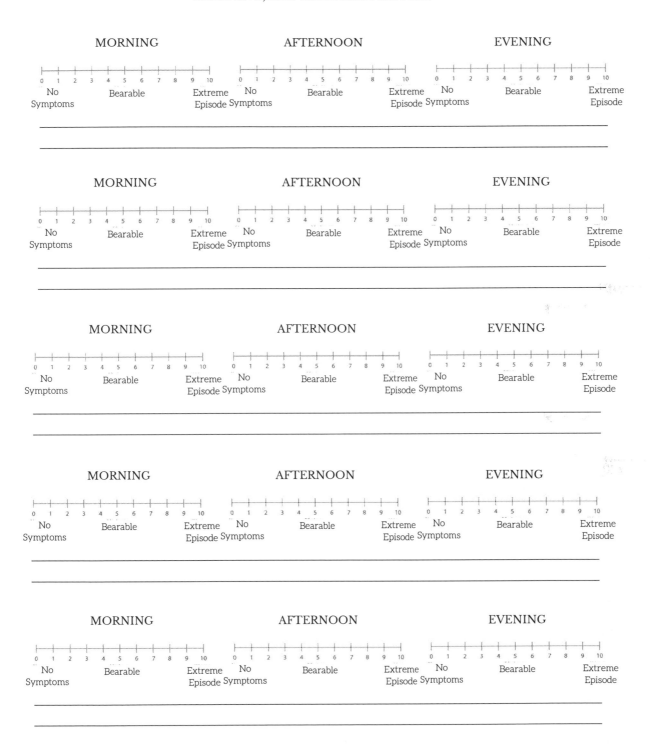

MORNING	AFTERNOON	EVENING
0 1 2 3 4 5 6 7 8 9 10	0 1 2 3 4 5 6 7 8 9 10	0 1 2 3 4 5 6 7 8 9 10
No Symptoms — Bearable — Extreme Episode	No Symptoms — Bearable — Extreme Episode	No Symptoms — Bearable — Extreme Episode

PAIN TRACKER BAR CHART

1
2
3
4
5
6
7
8
9
10

MONDAY	TUESDAY	WEDNESDAY	THURSDAY	FRIDAY	SATURDAY	SUNDAY

FOOD LOG AND FOOD TRIGGER TRACKER

FOOD	AMOUNT	TIME	IMMEDIATELY AFTER	1 HOUR	3 HOURS

LOG HOW YOU FEEL AFTER FOOD IN THESE SECTIONS

FOOD TRACKER

MEAL	MONDAY	TUESDAY	WEDNESDAY	THURSDAY	FRIDAY	SATURDAY	SUNDAY
BREAKFAST							
LUNCH							
DINNER							
CALORIES (OPTIONAL)							
SUPPLEMENTS	MULTIVIT ☐	MULTIVIT ☐	MULTIVIT ☐	MULTIVIT ☐	MULTIVIT ☐	MULTIVIT ☐	MULTIVIT ☐
	VITAMIN D ☐	VITAMIN D ☐	VITAMIN D ☐	VITAMIN D ☐	VITAMIN D ☐	VITAMIN D ☐	VITAMIN D ☐
	CALCIUM ☐	CALCIUM ☐	CALCIUM ☐	CALCIUM ☐	CALCIUM ☐	CALCIUM ☐	CALCIUM ☐
WATER INTAKE	☐☐☐ ☐☐☐	☐☐☐ ☐☐☐	☐☐☐ ☐☐☐	☐☐☐ ☐☐☐	☐☐☐ ☐☐☐	☐☐☐ ☐☐☐	☐☐☐ ☐☐☐

EXERCISE	MONDAY	TUESDAY	WEDNESDAY	THURSDAY	FRIDAY	SATURDAY	SUNDAY

FILL IN THE NOTES BELOW ON AREAS FOR IMPROVEMENT, SHOPPING LISTS, HOW YOU FELT AFTER YOU ATE, CALORIES, SNACKS AND WHATEVER YOU THINK WOULD BE USEFUL TO ADD TO YOUR FOOD JOURNAL

_____

_____

_____

_____

_____

_____

_____

_____

_____

HOW OFTEN DID YOU FILL OUT THIS CHART
NOT AT ALL   [ ]   1-3X PER WEEK   [ ]   ALMOST EVERY DAY   [ ]   EVERYDAY   [ ]

MEDICATION & SUPPLEMENT TRACKER

MEDICATION NAME	DOSE.	MON	TUES	WED	THURS	FRI	SAT	SUN
EXAMPLE	5mg							

_____

_____

_____

_____

_____

_____

_____

You are not a burden.
You HAVE a burden,
A burden is by its very
nature too heavy to carry
on it's own.

EXPLAIN WHY YOU ARE WORTHY OF LOVE AND DESERVE HAPPINESS.

ANSWER THESE QUESTIONS TO BREAK OUT OF NEGATIVE THOUGHT PATTERNS AND REFOCUS ON THE THINGS THAT MAKE YOU LOVE LIFE AND LOVE YOURSELF!

_____

_____

_____

_____

_____

_____

_____

_____

_____

_____

_____

_____

_____

_____

_____

_____

_____

_____

_____

_____

DAILY ENERGY vs MOOD TRACKER

TRACK YOUR DAILY ENERGY, MOOD AND ALSO PAIN USING DIFFERENT COLOURS ON THIS LINE CHART

100

75

50

25

0

ENERGY

| MONDAY | TUESDAY | WEDNESDAY | THURSDAY | FRIDAY | SATURDAY | SUNDAY |

PAIN

TIME OF DAY PAIN TRACKER

MORNING

```
0  1  2  3  4  5  6  7  8  9  10
```
No Pain   Moderate Pain   Worst Pain

AFTERNOON

```
0  1  2  3  4  5  6  7  8  9  10
```
No Pain   Moderate Pain   Worst Pain

EVENING

```
0  1  2  3  4  5  6  7  8  9  10
```
No Pain   Moderate Pain   Worst Pain

MORNING

```
0  1  2  3  4  5  6  7  8  9  10
```
No Pain   Moderate Pain   Worst Pain

AFTERNOON

```
0  1  2  3  4  5  6  7  8  9  10
```
No Pain   Moderate Pain   Worst Pain

EVENING

```
0  1  2  3  4  5  6  7  8  9  10
```
No Pain   Moderate Pain   Worst Pain

MORNING

```
0  1  2  3  4  5  6  7  8  9  10
```
No Pain   Moderate Pain   Worst Pain

AFTERNOON

```
0  1  2  3  4  5  6  7  8  9  10
```
No Pain   Moderate Pain   Worst Pain

EVENING

```
0  1  2  3  4  5  6  7  8  9  10
```
No Pain   Moderate Pain   Worst Pain

MORNING

```
0  1  2  3  4  5  6  7  8  9  10
```
No Pain   Moderate Pain   Worst Pain

AFTERNOON

```
0  1  2  3  4  5  6  7  8  9  10
```
No Pain   Moderate Pain   Worst Pain

EVENING

```
0  1  2  3  4  5  6  7  8  9  10
```
No Pain   Moderate Pain   Worst Pain

MORNING

```
0  1  2  3  4  5  6  7  8  9  10
```
No Pain   Moderate Pain   Worst Pain

AFTERNOON

```
0  1  2  3  4  5  6  7  8  9  10
```
No Pain   Moderate Pain   Worst Pain

EVENING

```
0  1  2  3  4  5  6  7  8  9  10
```
No Pain   Moderate Pain   Worst Pain

SYMPTOM & TRIGGER TRACKER

	FREQ. / SEVERITY Y/N	MON	TUES	WED	THURS	FRI	SAT	SUN
DID YOU HAVE A GOOD DAY? (YES NO, 0-5 BAD TO GOOD)	Y/N 0-5							
MUSCLE PAIN OR WEAKNESS	0-5							
JOINT PAIN	0-5							
ENERGY LEVELS	0-5							
ANXIETY	0-5							
DIFFICULTY SLEEPING	0-5							
FEELING DEPRESSED / LOW MOOD	0-5							
OVER SLEEPING	Y/N							
DROWSIENESS	0-5							
HEADACHE / MIGRAINE	Y/N							
NAUSEA	0-5							
DIARRHOEA	0-5							
CONSTIPATION	Y-N							
BLOATING	0-5							
ACID REFLUX	Y/N							
NUMBNESS OR TINGLING	0-5							
HAIR LOSS	0-5							
SWOLLEN LYMPH NODES	0-5							
HEART PALPITATIONS	Y/N							
DRY EYES OR VISION PROBLEMS	0-5							
RINGING IN EARS	Y/N							
SENSITIVITY TO LIGHT	0-5							
SENSITIVITY TO SOUND	Y/N							
FACIAL NUMBNESS	Y/N							
BRAIN FOG / DIFFICULTY CONCENTRATING	Y/N							
HEADACHE OR MIGRAINE	Y/N							

CONTINUE TO THE NEXT PAGE

SYMPTOM & TRIGGER TRACKER

	FREQ. / SEVERITY Y/N	MON	TUES	WED	THURS	FRI	SAT	SUN
EXERCISE	MINS							
RASH	0-5							
MOUTH SORES	Y/N							
SKIN RASH	0-5							
UTI, DARK URINE OR OTHER BLADDER ISSUES	0-5							
LOW GRADE FEVER	TEMP							
COLD OR INFECTION	Y/N							
SHORTNESS OF BREATH	Y/N							
MEDICATION:	DOSE	☐	☐	☐	☐	☐	☐	☐
MEDICATION:	DOSE							
MEDICATION:	DOSE							
MEDICATION:	DOSE							

FILL IN THE CHARTS TO TRACK SYMPTOMS AND THEN PUT DETAILS AND POST POSSIBLE TRIGGERS IN THE NOTES BELOW.

_____

_____

_____

_____

_____

_____

_____

_____

_____

_____

_____

_____

_____

HOW OFTEN DID YOU FILL OUT THIS CHART
NOT AT ALL   [ ]   1-3X PER WEEK   [ ]   ALMOST EVERY DAY   [ ]   EVERYDAY   [ ]

SYMPTOM TRACKER

DATE	TIME	DURATION	DESCRIPTION

TIME OF DAY SYMPTOM TRACKER

TRACK THE SEVERITY OF YOUR SYMPTOMS THROUGHOUT THE DAY USING THE
SCALE, USE THE NOTE SECTION BELOW TO LIST THE SYMPTOMS YOU EXPERIENCED.
USE THIS TO SEE IF CERTAIN TIMES OF DAY E.G. MEAL TIMES OR FIRST THING IN THE
MORNING, ARE TRIGGERS FOR YOU.

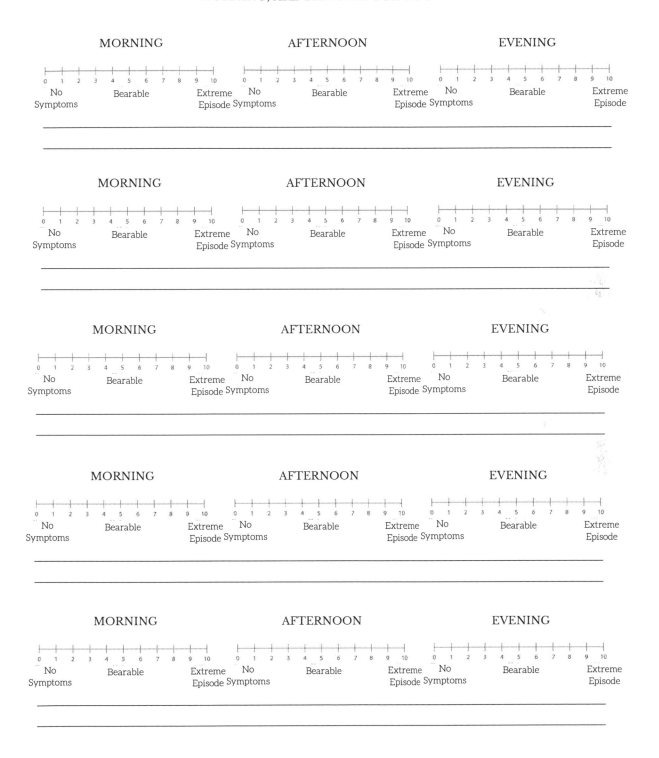

PAIN TRACKER BAR CHART

1

2

3

4

5

6

7

8

9

10

MONDAY	TUESDAY	WEDNESDAY	THURSDAY	FRIDAY	SATURDAY	SUNDAY

FOOD LOG AND FOOD TRIGGER TRACKER

FOOD	AMOUNT	TIME	IMMEDIATELY AFTER	1 HOUR	3 HOURS

LOG HOW YOU FEEL AFTER FOOD IN THESE SECTIONS

FOOD TRACKER

MEAL	MONDAY	TUESDAY	WEDNESDAY	THURSDAY	FRIDAY	SATURDAY	SUNDAY
BREAKFAST							
LUNCH							
DINNER							
CALORIES (OPTIONAL)							
SUPPLEMENTS	MULTIVIT ☐	MULTIVIT ☐	MULTIVIT ☐	MULTIVIT ☐	MULTIVIT ☐	MULTIVIT ☐	MULTIVIT ☐
	VITAMIN D ☐	VITAMIN D ☐	VITAMIN D ☐	VITAMIN D ☐	VITAMIN D ☐	VITAMIN D ☐	VITAMIN D ☐
	CALCIUM ☐	CALCIUM ☐	CALCIUM ☐	CALCIUM ☐	CALCIUM ☐	CALCIUM ☐	CALCIUM ☐
WATER INTAKE	☐☐☐☐ ☐☐☐☐	☐☐☐☐ ☐☐☐☐	☐☐☐☐ ☐☐☐☐	☐☐☐☐ ☐☐☐☐	☐☐☐☐ ☐☐☐☐	☐☐☐☐ ☐☐☐☐	☐☐☐☐ ☐☐☐☐

EXERCISE	MONDAY	TUESDAY	WEDNESDAY	THURSDAY	FRIDAY	SATURDAY	SUNDAY

FILL IN THE NOTES BELOW ON AREAS FOR IMPROVEMENT, SHOPPING LISTS, HOW YOU FELT AFTER YOU ATE, CALORIES, SNACKS AND WHATEVER YOU THINK WOULD BE USEFUL TO ADD TO YOUR FOOD JOURNAL

_____

_____

_____

_____

_____

_____

_____

_____

_____

HOW OFTEN DID YOU FILL OUT THIS CHART

NOT AT ALL   [ ]   1-3X PER WEEK   [ ]   ALMOST EVERY DAY   [ ]   EVERYDAY   [ ]

MEDICATION & SUPPLEMENT TRACKER

MEDICATION NAME	DOSE.	MON	TUES	WED	THURS	FRI	SAT	SUN
EXAMPLE	5mg							

_____

_____

_____

_____

_____

_____

_____

Be gentle with yourself.

You're doing the best you can.

Take every day as it comes.

DESCRIBE A TALENT YOU HAVE.

ANSWER THESE QUESTIONS TO BREAK OUT OF NEGATIVE
THOUGHT PATTERNS AND REFOCUS ON THE THINGS THAT MAKE
YOU LOVE LIFE AND LOVE YOURSELF!

EXPLAIN HOW YOU WILL FORGIVE YOURSELF FOR ANYTHING YOU FEEL SHAME OR REGRET ABOUT.

ANSWER THESE QUESTIONS TO BREAK OUT OF NEGATIVE THOUGHT PATTERNS AND REFOCUS ON THE THINGS THAT MAKE YOU LOVE LIFE AND LOVE YOURSELF!

_____

_____

_____

_____

_____

_____

_____

_____

_____

_____

_____

_____

_____

_____

_____

_____

_____

_____

_____

_____

DAILY ENERGY vs MOOD TRACKER

TRACK YOUR DAILY ENERGY, MOOD AND ALSO PAIN USING DIFFERENT COLOURS ON THIS LINE CHART

	MONDAY	TUESDAY	WEDNESDAY	THURSDAY	FRIDAY	SATURDAY	SUNDAY	
100								😁
75								🙂
50								😐
25								🙁
0								😦

ENERGY

PAIN

TIME OF DAY PAIN TRACKER

MORNING

0 1 2 3 4 5 6 7 8 9 10
No Pain   Moderate Pain   Worst Pain

AFTERNOON

0 1 2 3 4 5 6 7 8 9 10
No Pain   Moderate Pain   Worst Pain

EVENING

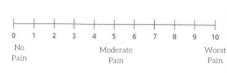

0 1 2 3 4 5 6 7 8 9 10
No Pain   Moderate Pain   Worst Pain

MORNING

0 1 2 3 4 5 6 7 8 9 10
No Pain   Moderate Pain   Worst Pain

AFTERNOON

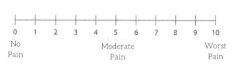

0 1 2 3 4 5 6 7 8 9 10
No Pain   Moderate Pain   Worst Pain

EVENING

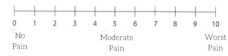

0 1 2 3 4 5 6 7 8 9 10
No Pain   Moderate Pain   Worst Pain

MORNING

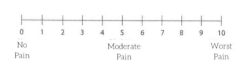

0 1 2 3 4 5 6 7 8 9 10
No Pain   Moderate Pain   Worst Pain

AFTERNOON

0 1 2 3 4 5 6 7 8 9 10
No Pain   Moderate Pain   Worst Pain

EVENING

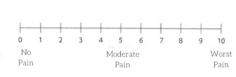

0 1 2 3 4 5 6 7 8 9 10
No Pain   Moderate Pain   Worst Pain

MORNING

0 1 2 3 4 5 6 7 8 9 10
No Pain   Moderate Pain   Worst Pain

AFTERNOON

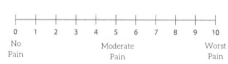

0 1 2 3 4 5 6 7 8 9 10
No Pain   Moderate Pain   Worst Pain

EVENING

0 1 2 3 4 5 6 7 8 9 10
No Pain   Moderate Pain   Worst Pain

MORNING

0 1 2 3 4 5 6 7 8 9 10
No Pain   Moderate Pain   Worst Pain

AFTERNOON

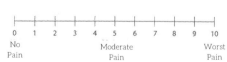

0 1 2 3 4 5 6 7 8 9 10
No Pain   Moderate Pain   Worst Pain

EVENING

0 1 2 3 4 5 6 7 8 9 10
No Pain   Moderate Pain   Worst Pain

SYMPTOM & TRIGGER TRACKER

	FREQ. / SEVERITY Y/N	MON	TUES	WED	THURS	FRI	SAT	SUN
DID YOU HAVE A GOOD DAY? (YES NO, 0-5 BAD TO GOOD)	Y/N 0-5	☐	☐	☐	☐	☐	☐	☐
MUSCLE PAIN OR WEAKNESS	0-5							
JOINT PAIN	0-5							
ENERGY LEVELS	0-5							
ANXIETY	0-5							
DIFFICULTY SLEEPING	0-5							
FEELING DEPRESSED / LOW MOOD	0-5							
OVER SLEEPING	Y/N							
DROWSIENESS	0-5							
HEADACHE / MIGRAINE	Y/N							
NAUSEA	0-5							
DIARRHOEA	0-5							
CONSTIPATION	Y-N							
BLOATING	0-5							
ACID REFLUX	Y/N							
NUMBNESS OR TINGLING	0-5							
HAIR LOSS	0-5							
SWOLLEN LYMPH NODES	0-5							
HEART PALPITATIONS	Y/N							
DRY EYES OR VISION PROBLEMS	0-5							
RINGING IN EARS	Y/N							
SENSITIVITY TO LIGHT	0-5							
SENSITIVITY TO SOUND	Y/N							
FACIAL NUMBNESS	Y/N							
BRAIN FOG / DIFFICULTY CONCENTRATING	Y/N							
HEADACHE OR MIGRAINE	Y/N							

CONTINUE TO THE NEXT PAGE

SYMPTOM & TRIGGER TRACKER

	FREQ. / SEVERITY Y/N	MON	TUES	WED	THURS	FRI	SAT	SUN
EXERCISE	MINS							
RASH	0-5							
MOUTH SORES	Y/N							
SKIN RASH	0-5							
UTI, DARK URINE OR OTHER BLADDER ISSUES	0-5							
LOW GRADE FEVER	TEMP							
COLD OR INFECTION	Y/N							
SHORTNESS OF BREATH	Y/N							
MEDICATION:	DOSE	☐	☐	☐	☐	☐	☐	☐
MEDICATION:	DOSE							
MEDICATION:	DOSE							
MEDICATION:	DOSE							

FILL IN THE CHARTS TO TRACK SYMPTOMS AND THEN PUT DETAILS AND POST POSSIBLE TRIGGERS IN THE NOTES BELOW.

_____
_____
_____
_____
_____
_____
_____
_____
_____
_____
_____
_____
_____
_____

HOW OFTEN DID YOU FILL OUT THIS CHART

NOT AT ALL   [ ]   1-3X PER WEEK   [ ]   ALMOST EVERY DAY   [ ]   EVERYDAY   [ ]

SYMPTOM TRACKER

DATE	TIME	DURATION	DESCRIPTION
DATE	TIME	DURATION	DESCRIPTION
DATE	TIME	DURATION	DESCRIPTION

TIME OF DAY SYMPTOM TRACKER

TRACK THE SEVERITY OF YOUR SYMPTOMS THROUGHOUT THE DAY USING THE
SCALE, USE THE NOTE SECTION BELOW TO LIST THE SYMPTOMS YOU EXPERIENCED.
USE THIS TO SEE IF CERTAIN TIMES OF DAY E.G. MEAL TIMES OR FIRST THING IN THE
MORNING, ARE TRIGGERS FOR YOU.

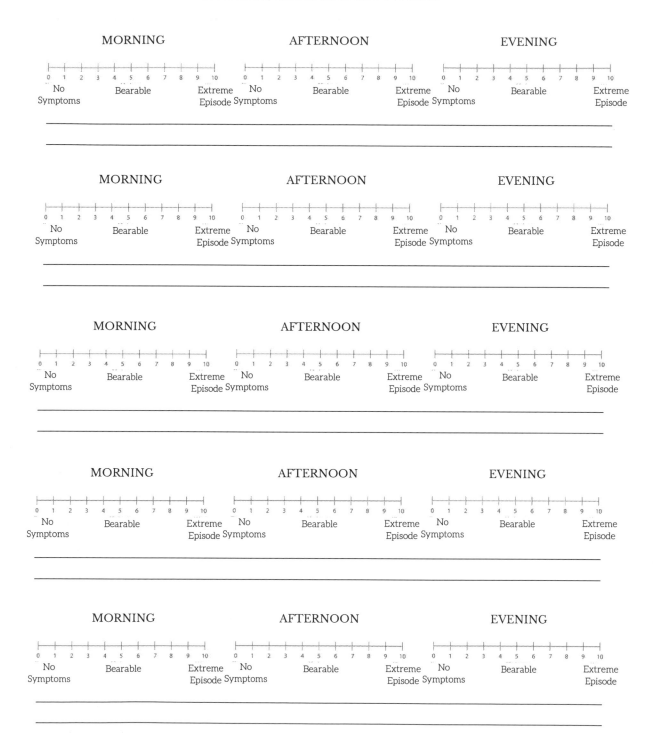

PAIN TRACKER BAR CHART

1

2

3

4

5

6

7

8

9

10

MONDAY	TUESDAY	WEDNESDAY	THURSDAY	FRIDAY	SATURDAY	SUNDAY

FOOD TRACKER

MEAL	MONDAY	TUESDAY	WEDNESDAY	THURSDAY	FRIDAY	SATURDAY	SUNDAY
BREAKFAST							
LUNCH							
DINNER							
CALORIES (OPTIONAL)							
SUPPLEMENTS	MULTIVIT ☐ VITAMIN D ☐ CALCIUM ☐	MULTIVIT ☐ VITAMIN D ☐ CALCIUM ☐	MULTIVIT ☐ VITAMIN D ☐ CALCIUM ☐	MULTIVIT ☐ VITAMIN D ☐ CALCIUM ☐	MULTIVIT ☐ VITAMIN D ☐ CALCIUM ☐	MULTIVIT ☐ VITAMIN D ☐ CALCIUM ☐	MULTIVIT ☐ VITAMIN D ☐ CALCIUM ☐
WATER INTAKE	☐☐☐☐ ☐☐☐☐	☐☐☐☐ ☐☐☐☐	☐☐☐☐ ☐☐☐☐	☐☐☐☐ ☐☐☐☐	☐☐☐☐ ☐☐☐☐	☐☐☐☐ ☐☐☐☐	☐☐☐☐ ☐☐☐☐

EXERCISE	MONDAY	TUESDAY	WEDNESDAY	THURSDAY	FRIDAY	SATURDAY	SUNDAY

FILL IN THE NOTES BELOW ON AREAS FOR IMPROVEMENT, SHOPPING LISTS, HOW YOU FELT AFTER YOU ATE, CALORIES, SNACKS AND WHATEVER YOU THINK WOULD BE USEFUL TO ADD TO YOUR FOOD JOURNAL

_____
_____
_____
_____
_____
_____
_____
_____
_____

HOW OFTEN DID YOU FILL OUT THIS CHART

NOT AT ALL   [ ]   1-3X PER WEEK   [ ]   ALMOST EVERY DAY   [ ]   EVERYDAY   [ ]

FOOD LOG AND FOOD TRIGGER TRACKER

LOG HOW YOU FEEL AFTER FOOD IN THESE SECTIONS

FOOD	AMOUNT	TIME	IMMEDIATELY AFTER	1 HOUR	3 HOURS

MEDICATION & SUPPLEMENT TRACKER

MEDICATION NAME	DOSE.	MON	TUES	WED	THURS	FRI	SAT	SUN
EXAMPLE	5mg							

SLEEP TRACKER

TOTAL SLEEP TIME	SLEEP START TIME	WAKE UP TIME	NAP TIMES	DATE

SLEEP TRACKER

TOTAL SLEEP TIME	SLEEP START TIME	WAKE UP TIME	NAP TIMES	DATE

SLEEP TRACKER

TOTAL SLEEP TIME	SLEEP START TIME	WAKE UP TIME	NAP TIMES	DATE

Made in United States
Orlando, FL
20 July 2022